职业教育改革创新示范教材

Qiche Zhuanye Yingyu
汽车专业英语

(第二版)

蔡北勤 主　　编
梁　楹 副 主 编
朱　军 丛书总主审

人民交通出版社股份有限公司
China Communications Press Co.,Ltd.

内 容 提 要

本书是职业教育改革创新示范教材之一。其主要内容包括：汽车基础英语、汽车发动机、汽车底盘、汽车电器、汽车维护与测试。

本书可作为职业院校汽车运用与维修专业的教学用书，也可供汽车维修及相关技术人员参考阅读。

图书在版编目(CIP)数据

汽车专业英语 / 蔡北勤主编. —2版. —北京：
人民交通出版社股份有限公司，2017.8
ISBN 978-7-114-14042-6

Ⅰ. ①汽… Ⅱ. ①蔡… Ⅲ. ①汽车工程—英语—中等专业学校—教材 Ⅳ. ①H31

中国版本图书馆 CIP 数据核字(2017)第 178095 号

职业教育改革创新示范教材
书　　名：	汽车专业英语（第二版）
著 作 者：	蔡北勤
责任编辑：	翁志新
出版发行：	人民交通出版社股份有限公司
地　　址：	(100011)北京市朝阳区安定门外外馆斜街3号
网　　址：	http://www.ccpress.com.cn
销售电话：	(010)59757973
总 经 销：	人民交通出版社股份有限公司发行部
经　　销：	各地新华书店
印　　刷：	北京市密东印刷有限公司
开　　本：	787×1092　1/16
印　　张：	10.5
字　　数：	240 千
版　　次：	2012 年 1 月　第 1 版 2017 年 8 月　第 2 版
印　　次：	2017 年 8 月　第 2 版　第 1 次印刷
书　　号：	ISBN 978-7-114-14042-6
定　　价：	24.00 元

(有印刷、装订质量问题的图书由本公司负责调换)

职业教育改革创新示范教材编委会

（排名不分先后）

主　　　任：刘建平（广州市交通运输职业学校）
　　　　　　杨丽萍（深圳市第二职业技术学校）
副　主　任：黄关山（珠海城市职业技术学院）　周志伟（深圳市宝安职业技术学校）
　　　　　　邱今胜（深圳信息职业技术学院）　朱小东（中山市沙溪理工学校）
　　　　　　侯文胜（佛山市顺德区中等专业学校）韩彦明（佛山市华材职业技术学校）
　　　　　　庞柳军（广州市交通运输职业学校）　程和勋（中山市中等专业学校）
　　　　　　冯　津（广州合赢教学设备有限公司）邱先贵（广东文舟图书发行有限公司）
委　　　员：谢伟钢、孟婕、王锋、曾艳（深圳市龙岗职业技术学校）
　　　　　　李博成（深圳市宝安职业技术学校）
　　　　　　罗雷鸣、陈根元、马征（惠州工业科技学校）
　　　　　　邱勇胜、何向东（清远市职业技术学校）
　　　　　　刘武英、陈德磊、阮威雄、江珠（阳江市第一职业技术学校）
　　　　　　苏小举、孙永江、李爱民（珠海市理工职业技术学校）
　　　　　　陈凡主（中山市沙溪理工学校）
　　　　　　刘小兵（广东省轻工高级职业技术学校）
　　　　　　许志丹、谭智男、陈东海、任丽（佛山市华材职业技术学校）
　　　　　　欧阳可良、马涛（佛山市顺德区中等专业学校）
　　　　　　周德新、张水珍（河源理工学校）
　　　　　　谢立梁（广州市番禺工贸职业技术学校）
　　　　　　范海飞、闫勇（广东省普宁职业技术学校）
　　　　　　温巧玉（广州市白云行知职业技术学校）
　　　　　　李维东、冯永亮、巫益平（佛山市顺德区郑敬怡职业技术学校）
　　　　　　王远明、郑新强（东莞理工学校）
　　　　　　程树青（惠州商业学校）
　　　　　　高灵聪（广州市信息工程职业学校）
　　　　　　黄宇林、邓津海（广东省理工职业技术学校）
　　　　　　张江生（湛江机电学校）
　　　　　　任家扬（中山市中等专业学校）
　　　　　　邹胜聪（深圳市第二职业技术学校）
丛书总主审：朱　军

第二版前言 PREFACE TO THE SECOND EDITION

"十二五"期间，人民交通出版社以职教专家、行业专家、学校教师、出版社编辑"四结合"的模式开发出了"职业教育改革创新示范教材"，受到广大职业院校师生的欢迎。

随着职业教育教学改革的不断深入，学校对课程、教材的内容与形式提出了更高的要求。《教育部关于深化职业教育教学改革全面提高人才培养质量的若干意见》（教职成〔2015〕6号）中提出：对接最新职业标准、行业标准和岗位规范，紧贴岗位实际工作过程，调整课程结构，更新课程内容，深化多种模式的课程改革。要普及推广项目教学、案例教学、情景教学、工作过程导向教学，广泛运用启发式、探究式、讨论式、参与式教学，充分激发学生的学习兴趣和积极性。根据文件精神，人民交通出版社股份有限公司组织专家和主编老师，对已出版的"职业教育改革创新示范教材"进行了全面修订，对个别不能完全适应学校教学的教材进行了重新整合，并增加了几种学校急需教材，更新了教材内容，并对教材中的错漏之处进行了修正。

《汽车专业英语》是其中一本，此次修订，纠正了第一版中的错误之处；更换了效果不佳的图片；增加了"车轮定位"和"世界技能竞赛"两节内容；删除了附录中的词汇表。

本书由蔡北勤担任主编，暨南大学的梁楹担任副主编，参加编写的还有鞠海鸥、林夏武、余鹏程、陈万春等。

职业教育改革创新示范教材编委会
2017年5月

第一版前言 / PREFACE

《国家中长期教育改革和发展规划纲要(2010—2020年)》中提出:大力发展职业教育,把职业教育纳入经济社会发展和产业发展规划,把提高质量作为重点;以服务为宗旨,以就业为导向,推进教育教学改革。实行工学结合、校企合作、顶岗实习的人才培养模式;满足人民群众接受职业教育的需求,满足经济社会对高素质劳动者和技能型人才的需要。

职业教育的发展已作为国家当前教育发展的战略重点之一,但目前学校所使用的教材普遍存在以下几个方面的问题:

(1) 学生反映难理解,教师反映不好教;

(2) 企业反映脱离实际,与他们的需求距离很大;

(3) 不适应新一轮教学改革的需要,汽车车身修复、汽车商务、汽车美容与装潢等专业教材急缺;

(4) 立体化程度不够,教学资源质量不高,教学方式相对落后。

针对以上问题,结合人民交通出版社汽车类专业教材的出版优势,我们开发了《职业教育改革创新示范教材》。本套教材以"积极探索教学改革思路,充分考虑区域性特点,提升学生职业素质"的指导思想,采用职教专家、行业一线专家、学校教师、出版社编辑"四结合"的编写模式。教材内容的特点是:准确体现职业教育特点(以工作岗位所需的知识和技能为出发点);理论内容"必需、够用";实训内容贴合工作一线实际;选图讲究,易懂易学。

该套教材将先进的教学内容、教学方法与教学手段有效地结合起来,形成课本、课件(部分课程配)和习题集(部分课程配)三位一体的立体教学模式。

本书由广州市交通运输职业学校蔡北勤担任主编,暨南大学梁楒担任副主编,参加编写的还有鞠海鸥、林夏武、余鹏程、陈万春等。

限于编者的经历和水平,书中难免有不妥或错误之处,敬请广大读者批评指正,提出修改意见和建议,以便再版修订时改正。

职业教育改革创新示范教材编委会
2011年5月

CONTENTS

Chapter 1　Automobile Basic English(汽车基础英语)　/1
- 1.1　Car Logo(车标) ················· 1
- 1.2　Classification of Vehicles(汽车的分类) ················· 4
- 1.3　Automobile Components(汽车的组成部分) ················· 7

Chapter 2　Automobile Engine(汽车发动机)　/10
- 2.1　The General Structure of an Engine(发动机总体构造) ················· 10
- 2.2　Inspect and Replace an Engine Coolant Temperature Sensor
  (检查与更换发动机冷却液温度传感器) ················· 17
- 2.3　Inspect Ignition System On-Vehicle(就车检查点火系统) ················· 22
- 2.4　Check Fuel Pressure(检查燃油压力) ················· 28
- 2.5　Remove and Install Crankshaft(拆卸与安装曲轴) ················· 33

Chapter 3　Automobile Chassis(汽车底盘)　/44
- 3.1　The General Structure of a Chassis(底盘的总体构造) ················· 44
- 3.2　Dismantle and Assemble Manual Transmission Input Shaft
  (拆卸和安装手动变速器输入轴) ················· 53
- 3.3　General Notes of AT Component Parts Removal
  (拆装自动变速器的注意事项) ················· 58
- 3.4　Install Front Axle Assembly(装配前桥总成) ················· 62
- 3.5　Remove and Install Power Steering Gear Box
  (拆卸和安装助力转向器) ················· 66

3.6 Remove and Install Brake Pads(拆卸和安装制动摩擦片) ……………………… 71

3.7 Wheel Alignment(车轮定位) ……………………………………………… 78

Chapter 4　Automobile Electric(汽车电器)　/83

4.1 The General Introduction of the Auto Electrical System

　　(汽车电气系统的总体介绍) ………………………………………………… 83

4.2 How to Use Electrical Equipments(如何使用电器设备) …………………… 91

4.3 Check and Adjust Headlight Settings(检查和调整前照灯设置) …………… 99

4.4 How to Read the Air Conditioning Wiring Diagram

　　(如何阅读空调电路图) ……………………………………………………… 105

4.5 The Introduction of the Night View Assist System

　　(夜视辅助系统的介绍) ……………………………………………………… 112

Chapter 5　Automobile Maintenance and Testing(汽车维护与测试)　/117

5.1 General Maintenance(日常维护) ………………………………………… 117

5.2 Change Engine Oil and Filter(更换机油和机油滤清器) ………………… 125

5.3 Diagnosis System(诊断系统) ……………………………………………… 130

5.4 Data List and Active Test(数据流和功能测试) …………………………… 135

5.5 The WorldSkills Competition(世界技能竞赛) …………………………… 142

Appendices(附录)　/148

Ⅰ Measuring Tools(各种工具量具) ………………………………………… 148

Ⅱ Abbreviations for Automobile(汽车常用缩略语) ………………………… 156

参考文献　/159

Chapter 1 Automobile Basic English
（汽车基础英语）

1.1　Car Logo(车标)

1. Do You Know These Car Logos?

Mercedes Benz(奔驰)	BMW(宝马)	Audi(奥迪)	Toyota(丰田)
Porsche(保时捷)	Lexus(雷克萨斯)	Rolls-Royce(劳斯莱斯)	Ferrari(法拉利)
FIAT(菲亚特)	Volkswagen(大众)	Suzuki(铃木)	Nissan(日产)
Lamborghini(兰博基尼)	Maybach(迈巴赫)	Bugatti(布加迪)	KIA(起亚)

Alfa-Romeo(阿尔法·罗密欧)　　Renault（雷诺）　　Aston Martin（阿斯顿·马丁）　　Cadillac（凯迪拉克）

Jaguar（捷豹）　　Lincoln（林肯）　　Chery（奇瑞）　　比亚迪

Dodge（道奇）　　Opel（欧宝）　　Ford（福特）　　Roewe（上汽荣威）

Honda（本田）　　Land Rover（路虎）　　Citroen（雪铁龙）　　Subaru（斯巴鲁）

Buick（别克）　　Bentley（宾利）　　Mitsubishi（三菱）　　长城

Hyundai（现代）　　Mazda（马自达）　　Chevrolet（雪佛兰）　　Chrysler（克莱斯勒）

GM（通用）　　Acura（阿库拉）　　Daewoo（大宇）　　Peugeot（标致）

Chapter 1 Automobile Basic English

2. Do You Know These Brands' Countries of Origin?

China _____

USA _____

Japan _____

British _____

French _____

Germany _____

Italy _____

Korea _____

3. Please Select One of These Famous Brands, and Tell the Story About It to The Others.

1.2 Classification of Vehicles(汽车的分类)

1. Cars Classification by Inner Space

One Box Car(一厢车)
　　一厢车是指车身为一个厢体的乘用车。发动机舱设在驾驶席的下面,与驾驶室一体化。车内空间宽敞,可存放多件行李物品。

Two Box Car(两厢车)
　　两厢车是指发动机舱和驾驶室分开的乘用车。在车辆发生正面碰撞时安全性很好,货物存放空间也很大。结合了一厢车和三厢车的优点。

Three Box Car(三厢车)
　　三厢车是指发动机舱、驾驶室、行李舱分开的乘用车,是乘用车最普通的外形。在车辆发生碰撞时,发动机舱、行李舱可以起到缓冲作用,因而安全性较好。

2. Cars Classification by Appearance

三厢轿车(Sedan)
　　乘用车的基本型,从廉价的大众车到高级的豪华车都得到广泛的应用。

双门轿跑车(Coupe)
　　追求奔跑乐趣的运动型跑车,比三厢车高度更低,一般设有两个车门。

掀背车(Hatchback Car)
　　车体后部设有向上开启的车门的小型两厢车。

Chapter 1　Automobile Basic English

运动型多用途车
（Sport Utility Vehicle,SUV）
　　可越野行驶，结构坚固，乘坐舒适的乘用车。

旅行车（Station Wagon）
　　采用三厢车设计的两厢车，行李舱和驾驶室为一体，提高货物存放能力。

皮卡（Pickup Truck）
　　车室前方有独立的发动机舱，后方可装载行李，是货车的一种。

厢式旅行车（Minivan）
　　两厢车的一种，有三排座椅和行李舱，属于车内空间宽敞的家庭用车。

敞篷车（Convertible）
　　车篷为开闭式或装卸式，又称为"Cabriolet"。

多用途车
（Multi Purpose Vehicle,MPV）
　　强调多功能性，是集轿车、旅行车和商务车于一身的车型。

3. Cars Classification by Drive Line

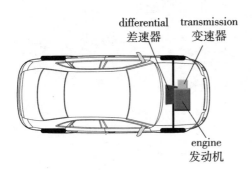
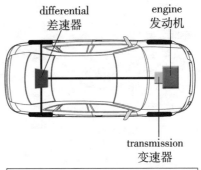

FF(front engine, front drive)
　　前置发动机和变速器，前轮驱动。

FR(front engine, rear drive)
　　前置发动机，后轮驱动。车厢下部必须安装传动轴。

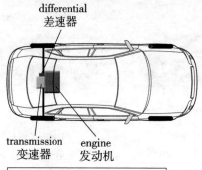

MR(middle engine, rear drive)
车厢和后轮车轴之间安置发动机，后轮驱动。

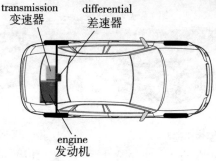

RR(rear engine, rear drive)
发动机和变速器安置在后轮车轴的后方，后轮驱动。

 Exercises(练习)

请选择正确的答案连线。

1. FF　　　　　　　　　　a. 后置后驱
2. FR　　　　　　　　　　b. 三厢轿车
3. SUV　　　　　　　　　c. 双门轿跑车
4. MPV　　　　　　　　　d. 前置前驱
5. Sedan　　　　　　　　e. 前置后驱
6. Convertible　　　　　f. 运动型多用途车
7. Coupe　　　　　　　　g. 敞篷车
8. RR　　　　　　　　　　h. 多用途车

1.3 Automobile Components(汽车的组成部分)

1. The Appearance of a Car

2. The Center Console

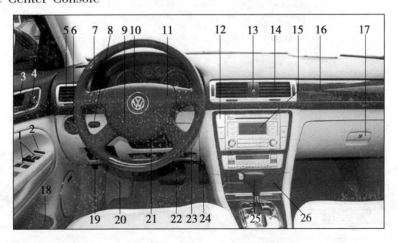

编号	英文	中文	编号	英文	中文
1	electrical window lifter switch	电动车窗玻璃升降器开关	15	radio	收音机
2	center control lock button	中央集控门锁按钮	16	copilot air bag	副驾驶人安全气囊
3	internal spanner	内开抠手	17	storage tank	储藏箱
4	rearview mirror regulator tap	后视镜调节开关	18	cup shelf	杯架
5,14	vent	出风口	19	engine cap unlock mechanism	发动机舱盖开锁装置
6	light switch	灯光开关	20	clutch pedal	离合器踏板
7	turn indicator system switch	转向信号灯开关	21	controlling shaft	转向盘高度调节控制杆
8	dashboard lighting control rotary knob	仪表盘照明调节旋钮	22	brake pedal	制动踏板
9	air bag	安全气囊	23	certificates and book storage tank	随车证书储存箱
10	clustered instrument board	组合式仪表盘	24	accelerate pedal	加速踏板
11	horn button	喇叭按钮	25	gear lever	换挡杆
12	rear window heater switch	后窗玻璃加热装置开关	26	car cigarette lighter	点烟器/插座
13	hazard warning light switch	危险警告灯开关			

3. Measurements

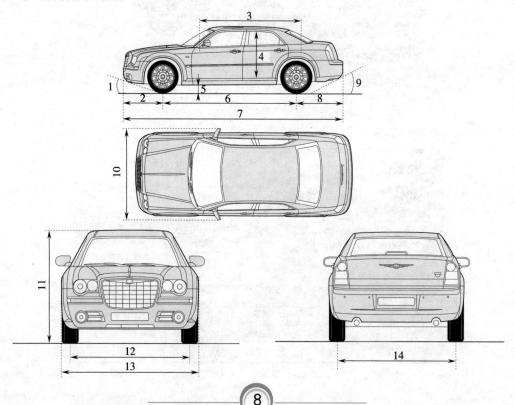

编号	英文	中文	编号	英文	中文
1	front overhang angle	接近角	8	rear overhang	后悬
2	front overhang	前悬	9	rear overhang angle	离去角
3	length of body	车厢长度	10	total width	总宽度
4	height of body	车厢高度	11	total height	总高度
5	ground clearance	离地间隙	12	front tire tread	前轮距
6	wheel space	轴距	13	width of body	车厢宽度
7	total length	总长度	14	rear tire tread	后轮距

4. Example of a Vehicle Specification Chart

Model(型号)	帕萨特(1.8T)	奔驰E300L时尚型
Dimension and Weight(尺寸及质量)		
Total Length(总长,mm)	4780	5012
Total Width(总宽,mm)	1740	1855
Total Height(总高,mm)	1470	1464
Trunk volume(行李舱容积,L)	475	540
Wheel Space(轴距,mm)	2803	3014
Complete Vehicle Kerb Mass(整备质量,kg)	1420	1845
Specification of Tire (Front)(前轮规格)	195/65R15	255/45R17
Specification of Tire (Rear)(后轮规格)	195/65R15	255/45R17
Engine(发动机)		
Cylinders(汽缸数)	L4	V6
Capacity(排气量,mL)	1781	2996
Nominal Power(额定功率,kW)	110/5700r/min	180/6000r/min
Nominal Torque(额定转矩,N·m)	210/1700r/min	300/2500~5000r/min
Compression Ratio(压缩比)	9.3	11.3
Full Speed(最高车速,km/h)	208	245
Type of Gear Box(变速器类型)	MT	AT
Tank Capacity(油箱容量,L)	62	80
Fuel Consumption of 100 km(百公里油耗,L)	7.3	10.4
Braking System/Suspension System/Drive line(制动系统/悬架/驱动方式)		
Braking System(Front/Rear)(制动系统 前/后)	通风盘	通风盘
Suspension System(Front)(前悬架系统)	多连杆式独立悬架	多连杆式独立悬架
Suspension System(Rear)(后悬架系统)	纵向托臂式扭力梁	多连杆式独立悬架
Drive Line(驱动方式)	FF	FR

Chapter 2 Automobile Engine
（汽车发动机）

2.1 The General Structure of an Engine
（发动机总体构造）

1. An Overview of a Gasoline Engine

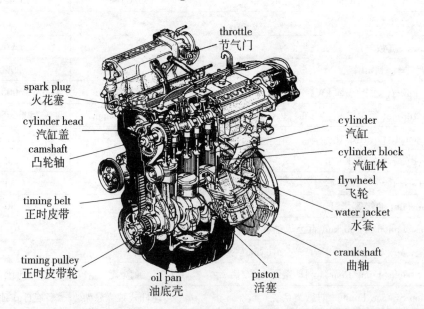

A gasoline engine is consist of the two mechanisms and the five systems.
(1) The two mechanisms.

Chapter 2　Automobile Engine

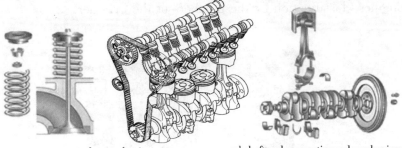

valve mechanism
配气机构

crankshaft and connecting rod mechanism
曲柄连杆机构

（2）The five systems.

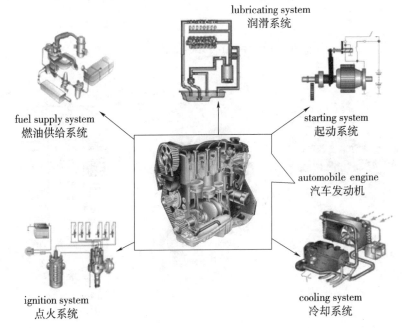

lubricating system
润滑系统

fuel supply system
燃油供给系统

starting system
起动系统

automobile engine
汽车发动机

ignition system
点火系统

cooling system
冷却系统

2. Engines Classification

（1）Engines classification by stroke.

two-stroke engine
二冲程发动机

four-stroke engine
四冲程发动机

(2) Engines classification by the numbers of the cylinder.

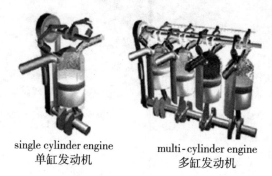

single cylinder engine
单缸发动机

multi-cylinder engine
多缸发动机

(3) Engines classification by cooling method.

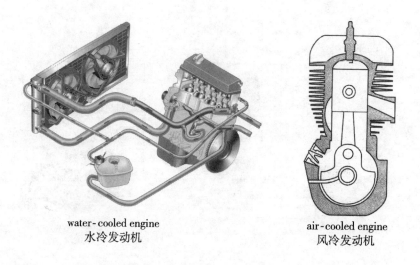

water-cooled engine
水冷发动机

air-cooled engine
风冷发动机

(4) Engines classification by cylinder arrangement.

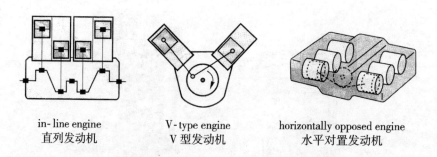

in-line engine
直列发动机

V-type engine
V 型发动机

horizontally opposed engine
水平对置发动机

(5) Engines classification by air Intake method.

Chapter 2   Automobile Engine

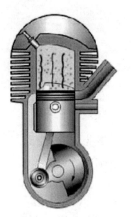
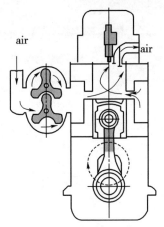

naturally aspirated engine
自然吸气发动机

supercharged engine
增压发动机

3. The Four Strokes of an Engine

intake stroke
进气行程

compression stroke
压缩行程

combustion stroke
作功行程

exhaust stroke
排气行程

 New Words(生词)

engine	发动机
structure	结构,构造
gasoline	汽油
throttle	节气门
camshaft	凸轮轴
cylinder	汽缸
flywheel	飞轮

crankshaft	曲轴
piston	活塞
mechanism	机构
stroke	行程,冲程
in-line	直列
horizontally	水平的
opposed	相反的
naturally	自然地
aspirated	送气的
supercharged	增压的
intake	进气
compression	压缩
combustion	燃烧,做功
exhaust	排气

Phrases(词组)

spark plug	火花塞
cylinder head	汽缸盖
cylinder block	汽缸体
timing belt	正时带
timing pulley	正时皮带轮
oil pan	油底壳
water jacket	水套
valve mechanism	配气机构
crank and connecting rod mechanism	曲柄连杆机构
cooling system	冷却系统
starting system	起动系统
ignition system	点火系统
fuel supply system	燃油供给系统
lubricating system	润滑系统

Chapter 2　Automobile Engine

intake stroke　　　　　　　　　　进气行程
compression stroke　　　　　　　压缩行程
combustion stroke　　　　　　　　做功行程
exhaust stroke　　　　　　　　　排气行程

Exercises(练习)

1. 把下面发动机构造图填写完整

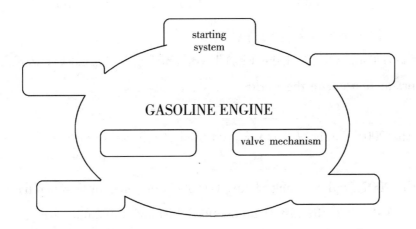

2. 给下面的示意图标记

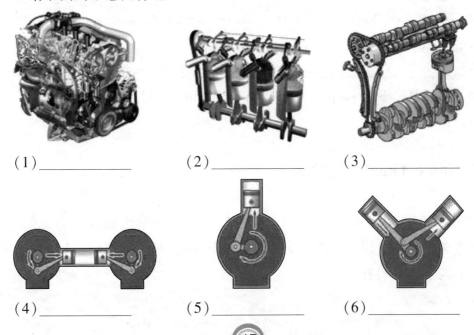

(1)_____　　(2)_____　　(3)_____

(4)_____　　(5)_____　　(6)_____

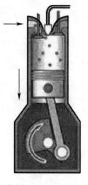 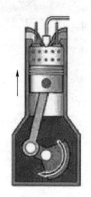  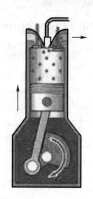

（7）_____　　（8）_____　　（9）_____　　（10）_____

3.用中文说出下列几款车的特点

（1）The 6.0-liter V-12 of the Enzo Ferrari makes it the most powerful naturally aspirated production car in the world.

特点：_____　_____　_____

（2）The 2008 Pontiac G8 is powered by a 361 horsepower V-8.

特点：_____

（3）The 2007 Ford Mustang Shelby GT500 is powered by a supercharged 5.4-liter twin cam V-8. It is the fastest production Mustang's engine.

特点：_____　_____　_____　_____
_____

（4）The Bugatti Veyron has a 16-cylinder monster engine with 4 turbochargers that produce 1001 horsepower！

特点：_____　_____　_____

（5）The BMW 7-Series packs a huge punch with a 450-hp 6.0-liter V-12.

特点：_____　_____　_____

 Game Time（游戏时间）

教师将写有英文或中文单词的卡片发给学生或由学生抽取其中一张，然后让该学生拿着卡片去找自己的朋友。中文或英文意思能和学生自己手中卡片意思吻合的同学就是朋友。

2.2 Inspect and Replace an Engine Coolant Temperature Sensor
（检查与更换发动机冷却液温度传感器）

1. Parts Location

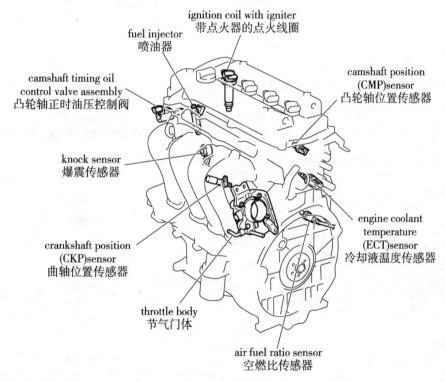

2. Removal

(1) Disconnect cable from negative battery terminal.

(2) Drain engine coolant.

(3) Remove engine coolant temperature sensor.

a. Disconnect the engine coolant temperature sensor connector.

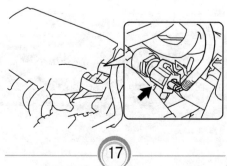

b. Using SST (Special Service Tools), remove the engine coolant temperature sensor.

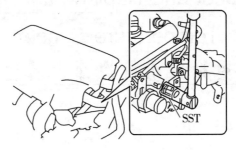

3. Inspection

Inspect engine coolant temperature sensor.

Check the resistance.

Using an ohmmeter, measure the resistance between the terminals, if the resistance is not as specified, replace the engine coolant temperature sensor.

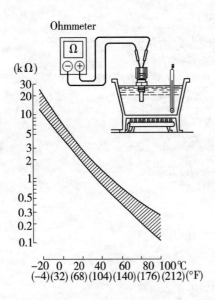

Standard resistance

Condition	Specified condition
Approximately 20℃	2.32~2.59kΩ
Approximately 80℃	0.310~0.326kΩ

NOTICE:

When checking the engine coolant temperature sensor in water, keep the terminals dry. After the check, wipe the sensor dry.

Chapter 2　Automobile Engine

Vocabulary

New Words（生词）

coolant	冷却液
temperature	温度
sensor	传感器
part	零件
igniter	点火器
valve	阀门
cable	电缆
negative	负极
battery	蓄电池
terminal	端子
drain	排干
connector	连接器
resistance	电阻
ohmmeter	欧姆表

Phrases（词组）

ignition coil	点火线圈
air fuel ratio sensor	空燃比传感器
throttle body	节气门体
knock sensor	爆震传感器
fuel injector	喷油器
camshaft timing oil control valve assembly	凸轮轴正时油压控制阀
CKP（crankshaft position sensor）	曲轴位置传感器
CMP（camshaft position sensor）	凸轮轴位置传感器
ECT（engine coolant temperature sensor）	发动机冷却液温度传感器
SST（Special Service Tools）	专用工具

汽车专业英语(第二版)

 Exercises(练习)

1. 根据课文内容,请重新编排检查更换发动机冷却液温度传感器的工作顺序

①断开蓄电池负极电缆;②使用专用工具拆卸发动机冷却液温度传感器;③检查发动机冷却液温度传感器电阻;④断开发动机冷却液温度传感器连接器;⑤排干发动机冷却液;⑥更换发动机冷却液温度传感器。

正确的顺序是:＿＿＿＿＿＿＿＿＿＿＿＿＿＿＿＿＿＿＿＿＿＿＿＿＿＿

2. 根据课文内容,回答以下问题

当检查水温为40℃时,发动机冷却液温度传感器的电阻范围是多少?如果检测得电阻值为2.5 kΩ,该传感器是否正常工作?试根据你的体会,说明发动机冷却液温度传感器的工作特点。

3. 翻译短文

When checking the engine coolant temperature sensor in water, keep the terminals dry. After the check, wipe the sensor dry.

4. 在下图中标明各元件的中英文名称

Chapter 2　Automobile Engine

 Game Time(游戏时间)

学生抽取一张写有冷却系统零部件英文单词的纸片,然后用中文描述这个零部件的功能、特点和它所在的位置,其他同学猜是哪个单词。如果哪位同学猜到,就说出该单词。

2.3 Inspect Ignition System On-Vehicle
（就车检查点火系统）

1. Parts Location

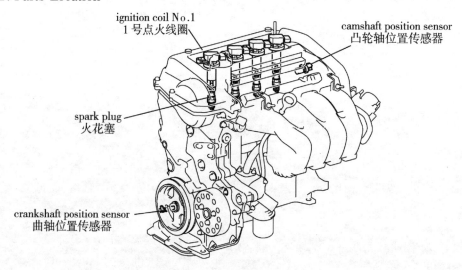

2. Inspect Ignition Coil and Spark Test

（1）Check for DTCs.

If a DTC is present, perform troubleshooting in accordance with the procedure for that DTC.

（2）Check whether sparks occur.

①Remove cylinder head cover No. 2.

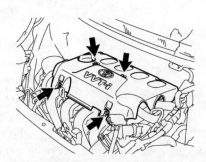

②Remove the 4 ignition coils.

a. Disconnect the 4 ignition coil connectors.

Chapter 2 Automobile Engine

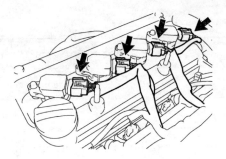

b. Remove the 4 bolts and 4 ignition coils.

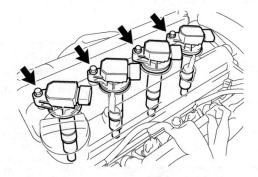

③Using a 16mm plug wrench, remove the 4 spark plugs.

④Install the spark plug onto each ignition coil and connect the ignition coil connectors.

⑤Disconnect the 4 injector connectors.

⑥Ground the spark plugs.

⑦Check that sparks occur while the engine is being cranked. (Do not crank the engine for more than 2 seconds). If sparks do not occur, perform the following procedure.

(3)Perform the spark test in accordance with the following procedure.

①Check that the wire harness connector of the ignition coil with igniter is securely connected.

Result	Proceed to
NG	Connect securely
OK	Go to next step

②Perform a spark test on each ignition coil with igniter.

a. Replace the ignition coil with igniter with a functioning one.

b. Perform the spark test again.

Result	Proceed to
NG	Replace ignition coil with igniter
OK	Go to next step

③Check that the power is supplied to the ignition coil with igniter.

a. Turn the engine switch on.

b. Check that the battery voltage is applied to the positive (+) terminal of the ignition coil.

Result	Proceed to
NG	Check wiring between ignition switch and ignition coil with igniter
OK	Go to next step

④Check the resistance of the camshaft position sensor.

Result	Proceed to
NG	Replace camshaft position sensor
OK	Go to next step

⑤Check the resistance of the crankshaft position sensor.

Result	Proceed to
NG	Replace crankshaft position sensor
OK	Go to next step

⑥Check the IGT from the ECM.

Result	Proceed to
NG	Check ECM
OK	Repair wiring between ignition coil and ECM

(4) Connect the 4 injector connectors.

(5) Using a 16mm plug wrench, install the 4 spark plugs. (Torque:18N·m)

(6) Install the 4 ignition coils.

(7) Install cylinder head cover No.2.

Chapter 2　Automobile Engine

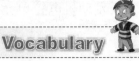

 New Words(生词)

ignition	点火
system	系统
vehicle	车辆
coil	线圈
spark	火花
perform	执行
troubleshooting	故障排除
procedure	步骤
cover	罩子
bolt	螺栓
plug	塞子
wrench	扳手
injector	喷油器
ground	接地,搭铁
switch	开关
positive	正极
torque	转矩

 Phrases(词组)

DTC	故障码
in accordance with	依照,与…一致
cylinder head cover	汽缸盖罩
wire harness	线束
ignition switch	点火开关

IGT   点火控制信号
ECM   发动机电控单元

 Exercises(练习)

1. 根据课文内容,请用中文叙述火花测试的步骤
①拆除 2 号汽缸盖罩;
②拆除 4 个点火线圈;
③_____;
④_____;
⑤断开 4 个喷油器连接器;
⑥_____;
⑦运转曲轴,检查火花塞是否跳火。

2. 根据课文内容,完成以下检修的流程图

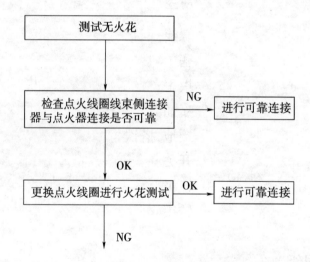

3. 下图显示为ECM端子分布情况,参照示例,完成填空

Symbols(Terminal No)	Wiring colors	Descriptions	Conditions	Specified Conditions
BATT(A21-20)-E1(C20-104)	Y-W	Battery	Always	11 to 14V
+B(A21-2)-E1(C20-104)	B-W	Power source of ECM	Ignition switch ON	11 to 14V
G2+(C20-99)-NE-(C20-121)	B-P	Camshaft position sensor	Idling	Pulse generation
NE+(C20-122)-NE-(C20-121)	L-P	Crankshaft position sensor	Idling	Pulse generation
…	…	…	…	…

蓄电池(BATT)对应A21插头的端子20,所以蓄电池(BATT)为A21-20。搭铁_____,凸轮轴位置传感器_____,曲轴位置传感器_____。

 Game Time(游戏时间)

全班分成若干小组。每组选一位代表站到教室前,老师发给其他同学一张印有汽车专业英语词汇的卡片。小组每个成员轮流把自己记住的单词口头拼写给选出的代表并告诉他该单词的意思。小组代表把单词和单词的意义写在空白卡片上。游戏结束时,完成最多的小组胜出。

2.4 Check Fuel Pressure(检查燃油压力)

1. Parts Location

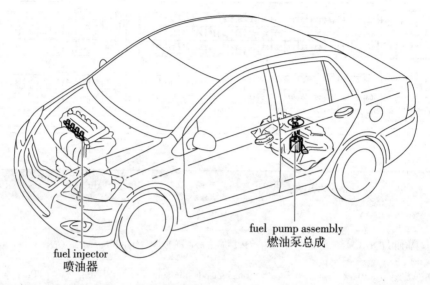

fuel pump assembly
燃油泵总成

fuel injector
喷油器

2. Discharge Fuel System Pressure

CAUTION:

Before removing any fuel system parts, take precautions to prevent gasoline spillage.

As some pressure remains in the fuel line even after taking precautions to prevent gasoline spillage, use a shop rag or piece of cloth to prevent gasoline splashes when disconnecting the fuel line.

(1) Remove the rear seat cushion.
(2) Remove the rear floor service hole cover.
(3) Disconnect the connector from the fuel pump assembly.

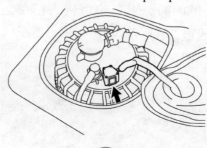

(4) Start the engine. After the engine stops naturally, turn the ignition switch off.

(5) Crank the engine again and make sure that the engine does not start.

(6) Remove the fuel tank cap and discharge the pressure.

(7) Disconnect the cable from the negative battery terminal.

(8) Connect the connector of the fuel pump assembly.

3. Check Fuel Pressure

(1) Discharge the fuel system pressure.

(2) Using a voltmeter, measure the battery voltage.

Standard voltage: 11~14V.

(3) Disconnect the negative (-) battery terminal cable.

(4) Remove fuel pipe clamp No.1 from the fuel tube connector.

(5) Disconnect the fuel hose from the fuel main tube.

(6) Install SST(pressure gauge and fuel tube connector).

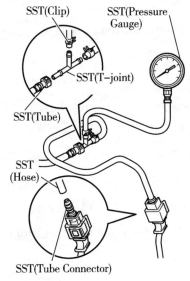

(7) Wipe off any spilt gasoline.

(8) Reconnect the negative (-) battery terminal cable.

(9) Connect the intelligent tester to the DLC3.

① Turn the ignition switch on and the intelligent tester main switch on.

NOTICE:
Do not start the engine.

②Select the Active Test mode on the intelligent tester.

HINT：Refer to the intelligent tester operator's manual for further details.

(10) Measure the fuel pressure.

Fuel pressure：304~343 kPa (3.1~3.5 kgf/cm^2).

If the pressure is high, replace the fuel pressure regulator.

If the pressure is low, check the fuel hoses, fuel hose connections, fuel pump and fuel pressure regulator.

(11) Disconnect the intelligent tester from the DLC3.

(12) Start the engine.

(13) Measure the fuel pressure while the engine is idling.

Fuel pressure：304~343 kPa (3.1~3.5 kgf/cm^2).

If the pressure is not as specified, check the vacuum sensing hose and the fuel pressure regulator.

(14) Stop the engine.

(15) Check that the fuel pressure remains as specified for 5 minutes after the engine stops.

Fuel pressure：147 kPa (1.5 kgf/cm^2) or more.

If the pressure is not as specified, check the fuel pump, pressure regulator and injectors.

(16) After checking the fuel pressure, disconnect the negative (-) battery terminal cable and carefully remove SST to prevent gasoline splashes.

(17) Reconnect the fuel tube to the fuel main tube.

(18) Install fuel pipe clamp No.1 onto the fuel tube connector.

(19) Check for fuel leakage.

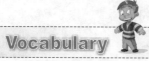

 New Words(生词)

| discharge | 释放 |
| fuel | 燃油 |

pressure	压力
cushion	垫子
tank	箱
cap	盖
hose	软管
regulator	调节器
idling	怠速
vacuum	真空
leakage	泄漏

Phrases(词组)

fuel pump	油泵
fuel tank cap	油箱盖
fuel pipe	油管
intelligent tester	解码器
fuel pressure regulator	燃油压力调节器

Exercises(练习)

1. 英译汉

(1) Start the engine, after the engine stops naturally, turn the ignition switch OFF.

(2) Disconnect the cable from the negative battery terminal.

(3) If the pressure is low, check the fuel hoses, fuel hose connections, fuel pump and fuel pressure regulator.

(4) Measure the fuel pressure while the engine is idling.

(5) Check that the fuel pressure remains as specified for 5 minutes after the engine stops.

_____

2. 根据课文内容,请用中文叙述释放燃油压力的步骤,并分析释放燃油压力的原因

_____

_____

_____

3. 根据课文内容判断下列描述是否正确

(1) There is no pressure remain after taking precautions to prevent gasoline spillage. ( )

(2) Before check fuel pressure, discharging the fuel system pressure is necessary. ( )

(3) If the pressure is high, check the fuel pump and fuel pressure regulator. ( )

(4) After checking the fuel pressure, carefully remove SST to prevent gasoline splashes. ( )

Game Time(游戏时间)

请使用下列字母拼写相应的专业词汇,每使用一个字母得一分,每个字母限用一次,相同的字母可使用的最多次数按该字母的给定次数,如字母 a 最多可使用两次,字母 i 最多可使用三次等。得分最多的同学胜出。

a a b c d e e f g h i i i k l m n n o r s t t u y

例:fuel 共使用4个字母,得4分。

2.5 Remove and Install Crankshaft

（拆卸与安装曲轴）

1. Parts Location

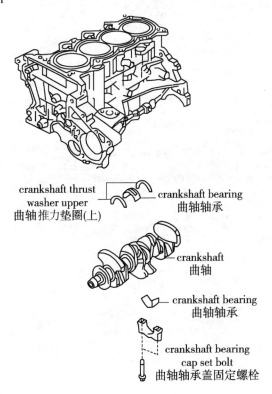

2. Disassembly

（1）Remove spark plug.

（2）Remove knock sensor and engine oil pressure switch assembly.

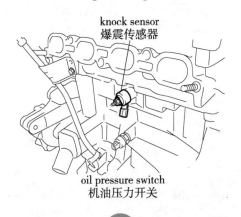

(3) Remove engine coolant temperature sensor.

(4) Remove water inlet and thermostat.

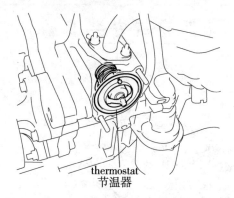

thermostat
节温器

(5) Remove oil filler cap sub-assembly.

(6) Remove crankshaft position sensor.

(7) Remove cylinder head cover sub-assembly.

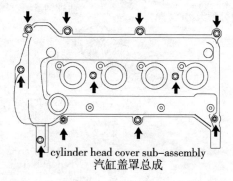

cylinder head cover sub-assembly
汽缸盖罩总成

(8) Remove camshaft timing oil control valve assembly.

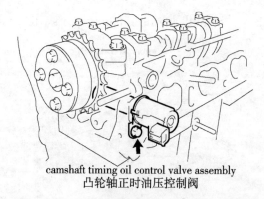

camshaft timing oil control valve assembly
凸轮轴正时油压控制阀

(9) Remove water pump pulley.

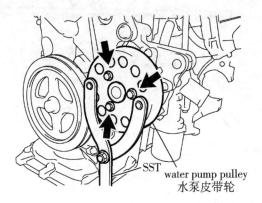

(10) Remove crankshaft damper sub-assembly.

①Set cylinder No. 1 to TDC/compression.

a. Turn the crankshaft damper sub-assembly, and align its timing notch with timing mark "0" of the oil pump.

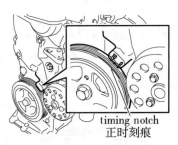

b. Check that the timing marks on the camshaft timing sprocket and the camshaft timing gear are all facing upward.

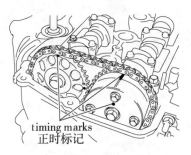

If not, turn the crankshaft complete revolution(360°) and align the marks as above.

②Using 2 SSTs, loosen the bolt while holding the crankshaft damper sub-assembly.

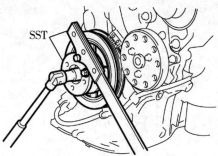

③Remove the crankshaft damper sub-assembly.

(11) Remove transverse engine mounting bracket.

(12) Remove water pump assembly.

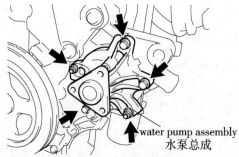

water pump assembly
水泵总成

(13) Remove oil pump assembly.

(14) Remove chain tensioner assembly.

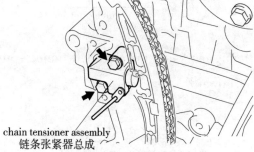

chain tensioner assembly
链条张紧器总成

(15) Remove chain tensioner slipper, chain vibration damper and chain sub- assembly.

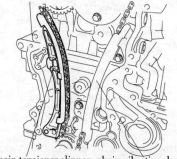

chain tensioner slipper   chain vibration damper
链条张紧器导轨   链条减振器

(16) Remove fuel delivery pipe sub- assembly.

(17) Remove camshaft position sensor.

(18) Remove No. 2 camshaft.

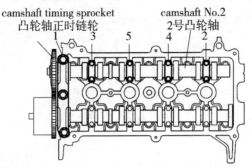

NOTICE:

When rotating the camshaft with the timing chain removed, rotate the crankshaft counterclockwise 40° from the TDC first.

Using several steps, uniformly loosen and remove the 11 bearing cap bolts in the sequence shown in the illustration, then remove camshaft bearing cap and camshaft No. 2.

NOTICE:

Loosen each bolt uniformly while keeping the camshaft level.

(19) Remove camshaft timing sprocket.

(20) Remove camshaft.

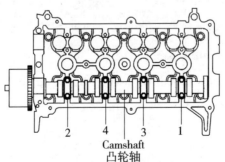

Using several steps, uniformly loosen and remove the 8 bearing cap bolts in the sequence shown in the illustration, then remove camshaft bearing cap and the camshaft.

> **NOTICE:**
> Loosen each bolt uniformly while keeping the camshaft level.

(21) Remove cylinder head sub-assembly.

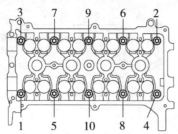

Using several steps, uniformly loosen and remove the 10 cylinder head bolts with an 8 mm bi-hexagon wrench in the sequence shown in the illustration, then remove the 10 cylinder head bolts and the plate washers.

> **NOTICE:**
> Do not drop the washers into the cylinder head.
> Head warpage or cracking could result from removing bolts in the wrong order.

(22) Remove oil filter sub-assembly.

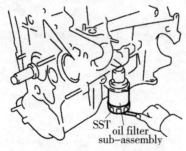

(23) Remove oil pan sub-assembly.

(24) Remove piston sub-assembly with connecting rod.

①Using a ridge reamer, remove all the carbon from the top of the cylinder.

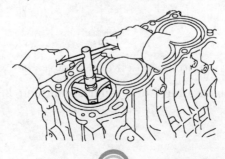

②Push the piston, connecting rod assembly and upper bearing down through the top of the cylinder block to remove them.

HINT:
Keep the bearing, connecting rod and cap together.
Keep the piston and the connecting rod assemblies in the correct order so that they can be returned to their original locations when reassembled.

(25) Remove connecting rod bearing.

(26) Remove crankshaft and crankshaft bearing.

①Using several steps, loosen and remove the 10 bearing cap sub-assembly bolts uniformly with SST in the sequence shown in the illustration.

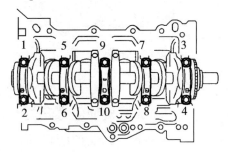

②Remove the bearing cap and the crankshaft.

(27) Install in the reverse order.

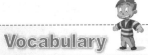

New Words(生词)

thermostat	节温器
assembly	装配,总成
pump	泵
pulley	皮带轮
damper	减振器
align	对齐
notch	刻痕

mark	标记
sprocket	链轮
gear	齿轮
transverse	横向
tensioner	张紧器
slipper	滑轨
chain	链条
bearing	轴承
block	箱体
washer	垫圈
warpage	翘曲
cracking	破裂

Phrases（词组）

oil pressure switch	机油压力开关
oil filler cap	机油加注口盖
sub-assembly	分部总成
mounting bracket	安装支架
chain tensioner	链条张紧器
fuel delivery pipe	燃油分配管

Exercises（练习）

1. 英译汉

(1) Turn the crankshaft damper sub-assembly, and align its timing notch with timing mark "0" of the oil pump.

(2) Check that the timing marks on the camshaft timing sprocket and the camshaft timing gear are all facing upward, as shown in the illustration.

(3) Using several steps, uniformly loosen and remove the 10 cylinder head bolts with an 8 mm bi-hexagon wrench in the sequence shown in the illustration, then remove the 10 cylinder head bolts and the plate washers

_____

(4) Using a ridge reamer, remove all the carbon from the top of the cylinder.

_____

(5) Keep the piston and the connecting rod assemblies in the correct order so that they can be returned to their original locations when reassembled.

_____

2. 写出下列零部件的英文名称

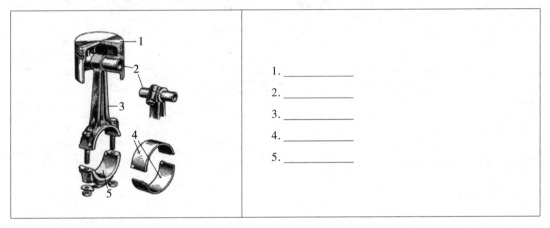

1. _____
2. _____
3. _____
4. _____
5. _____

3. 阅读某网店一则奥迪汽车发动机零部件英文价目表,然后填写相应的答案

Audi Engine Parts

Balance shaft assembly				
Balance shaft assembly Parts	Dealer Price	Our Price	Savings	
A6-3.2L (V6)	$ 122.98	$ 84.86	$ 38.12	ADD TO CART
Camshaft & timing				
Camshaft & timing Parts	Dealer Price	Our Price	Savings	
Camshaft left-3.2L (V6)	$ 836.21	$ 644.30	$ 191.91	ADD TO CART
Camshaft seal A6-3.2L (V6)	$ 6.78	$ 4.68	$ 2.10	ADD TO CART
Sprocket #3-3.2L (V6)	$ 235.90	$ 162.77	$ 73.13	ADD TO CART

续上表

Crankshaft & bearings				
Crankshaft & bearings Parts	Dealer Price	Our Price	Savings	
Bearings-4.2L(V8)	$24.32	$16.78	$7.54	ADD TO CART
Gasket A6-4.2L(V8)	$19.88	$13.72	$6.16	ADD TO CART
Cylinder block				
Cylinder block Parts	Dealer Price	Our Price	Savings	ADD TO CART
-3.2L(V6)	$2387.07	$2058.86	$328.21	ADD TO CART
Cylinder head & valves				
Cylinder head & valves Parts	Dealer Price	Our Price	Savings	
Cylinder head left-3.2L(V6)	$2309.87	$1992.27	$317.60	ADD TO CART
Rocker arms A6-3.2L(V6)	$16.85	$11.63	$5.22	ADD TO CART
Valve lifters A6-3.2L(V6)	$16.62	$11.47	$5.15	ADD TO CART
Valve seals A6-3.2L(V6)	$7.25	$5.00	$2.25	ADD TO CART
Valve springs A6-3.2L(V6)	$16.13	$11.13	$5.00	ADD TO CART
Lubrication				
Oil pump A6-3.2L(V6)	$267.95	$184.89	$83.06	ADD TO CART
Oil cooler A6-3.2L(V6)	$283.90	$195.89	$88.01	ADD TO CART
Mounts				
Mounts Parts	Dealer Price	Our Price	Savings	
Mount support -3.2L(V6)	$61.05	$42.12	$18.93	ADD TO CART
Pistons, rings & bearings				
Pistons, rings & bearings Parts	Dealer Price	Our Price	Savings	
Bearings Lower-3.2L(V6)	$9.42	$6.50	$2.92	ADD TO CART
Connecting rod A6-3.2L(V6)	$929.84	$716.44	$213.40	ADD TO CART
Piston-3.2L(V6)	$398.85	$275.21	$123.64	ADD TO CART
Piston ring set-3.2L(V6)	$95.48	$65.88	$29.60	ADD TO CART

(1) 用中文表述本价目表所罗列发动机的零部件种类。

(2) 奥迪4.2L(V8)曲轴轴瓦的市场一般售价是：

(3) 客商A需要四套奥迪3.2L(V6)摇臂，若从本网店购进，他将要支付：

(4)客商B已从本网店购得多件3.2L（V6）正时链轮,每件正时链轮他可以省下：

_____。

(5)客商C打算在本网店购进一批奥迪发动机零部件,它们分别是3.2L（V6）气门挺柱及油封各一个,油泵2个,活塞环6组。那么,客商C总共只需支出：

_____。

Game Time（游戏时间）

根据横向和纵向的图片圈出网格里相应汽车零部件的英文名称。

横向：

纵向：

h	d	a	s	u	m	p	y	f	a	g
e	b	o	p	v	e	i	n	l	r	a
w	e	b	o	l	t	s	z	y	e	b
g	a	s	k	e	t	e	w	h	e	e
u	r	w	i	y	o	o	m	h	a	l
n	i	c	y	l	i	n	d	e	r	e
i	n	o	y	x	m	a	r	e	i	v
k	g	s	i	m	u	k	j	l	n	q
q	s	e	e	r	f	l	a	n	g	e

Chapter 3 Automobile Chassis

(汽车底盘)

3.1 The General Structure of a Chassis
(底盘的总体构造)

1. An Overview of a Chassis

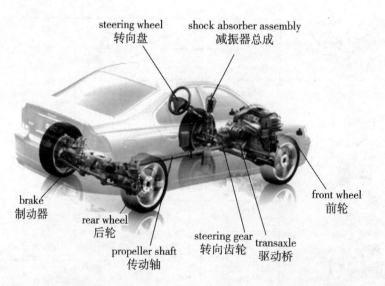

A chassis is consist of the transmission system, the driving system, the steering system and the brake system.

Chapter 3 Automobile Chassis

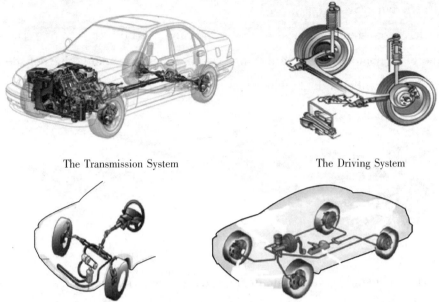

The Transmission System

The Driving System

The Steering System

The Brake System

2. The Transmission System

The transmission system is consist of the clutch, the manual transmission or the automatic transmission and the drive axle.

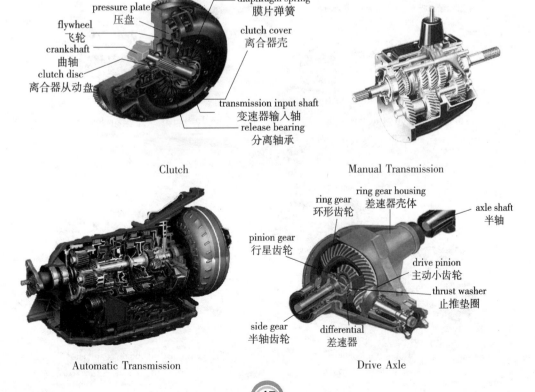

Clutch

Manual Transmission

Automatic Transmission

Drive Axle

3. The Driving System

The driving system is consist of the suspension, the tire and so on. The suspension is the main component of the driving system. There are many types of the suspension, such as the independent suspension and the dependent suspension.

Independent Suspension

Dependent Suspension

(1) The independent suspension can be divided into the macpherson strut suspension, the torsion beam suspension, the multi-link suspension, the double wishbone suspension and the active suspension.

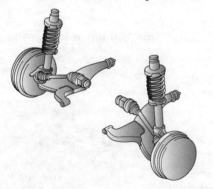
The Macpherson Strut Suspension

The Torsion Beam Suspension

The Multi-Link Suspension

The Double Wishbone Suspension

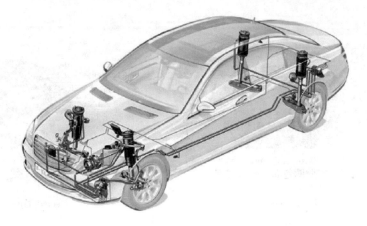

The Active Suspension

(2) The dependent suspension can be divided into the coil spring independent suspension, the pneumatic spring independent suspension and the steel plate spring independent suspension.

The Coil Spring Independent Suspension   The Pneumatic Spring Independent Suspension

The Steel Plate Spring Independent Suspension

(3) The tire is another important component of the driving system. There are two types of the tire: the radial tire and the diagonal tire.

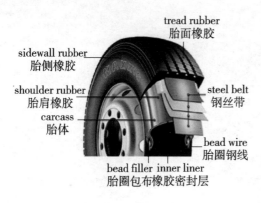
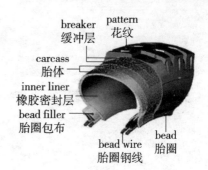

Radial Tire   Diagonal Tire

4. The Steering System

The steering system can be divided into the mechanical steering system and the power steering system. There are two types of the power steering system: the hydraulic power steering system and the electronic power steering system.

5. The Brake System

The brake system can be divided into the service brake system and the parking brake system.

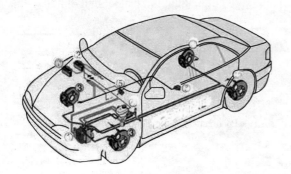
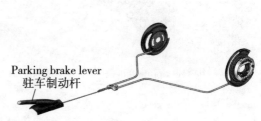

The Service Brake System   The Parking Brake System

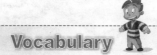

New Words(生词)

chassis   底盘

steering	转向
wheel	车轮
suspension	悬架
propeller	推进器
shaft	轴
transaxle	驱动桥
absorber	减振器
transmission	变速器
brake	制动
clutch	离合器
pinion	小齿轮
differential	差速器
tire	轮胎
spring	弹簧
pneumatic	气动的
tread	胎面
rubber	橡胶
breaker	缓冲层
pattern	花纹
carcass	胎体
sidewall	胎侧
shoulder	胎肩
hydraulic	液压的
electronic	电子的

Phrases(词组)

driving wheel	驱动车轮
propeller shaft	传动轴
shock absorber assembly	减振器总成

lower suspension arm	下悬架臂
front wheel	前轮
rear wheel	后轮
driving system	行驶系
manual transmission	手动变速器
automatic transmission	自动变速器
independent suspension	独立悬架
dependent transmission	非独立悬架
macpherson strut suspension	麦弗逊悬架
torsion beam suspension	扭力梁悬架
multi-link suspension	多连杆悬架
double wishbone suspension	双叉臂悬架
active suspension	主动悬架
elastic component	弹性元件
coil spring	螺旋弹簧
diaphragm spring	膜片弹簧
clutch disc	离合器片
thrust bearing	推力轴承
release bearing	分离轴承
pressure plate	压盘
torsional absorber	扭转减振器
pneumatic spring	空气弹簧
steel slate spring	钢板弹簧
radial tire	子午线轮胎
diagonal tire	斜交轮胎
service brake	行车制动
parking brake(hand brake)	驻车制动

 Exercises(练习)

1. 把下面底盘构造图填写完整

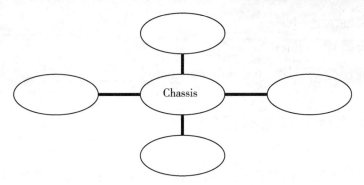

2. 给下面的示意图标记

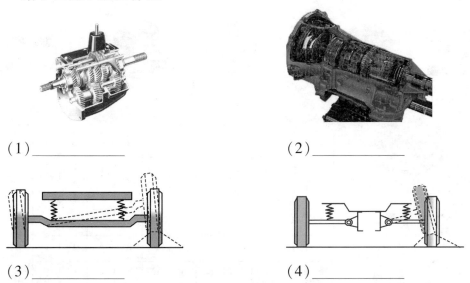

(1)＿＿＿＿＿＿＿   (2)＿＿＿＿＿＿＿

(3)＿＿＿＿＿＿＿   (4)＿＿＿＿＿＿＿

3. 根据中文提示,用方框里的词填空,组成汽车术语

housing　output　spring　wheel　gear　tyre　shaft　disc　bearing　module

(1) 液力变矩器壳　torque converter ＿＿＿＿＿＿

(2) 输出轴　＿＿＿＿＿＿ shaft

(3) 螺旋弹簧　coil ＿＿＿＿＿＿

(4) 转向盘　steering ＿＿＿＿＿＿

(5) 半轴　axle ＿＿＿＿＿＿

(6) 转向器　steering ＿＿＿＿＿＿

(7) 行星齿轮　pinion ＿＿＿＿＿＿

(8) 子午线轮胎　radial ＿＿＿＿＿＿

(9) 后轮　rear ＿＿＿＿＿＿

(10) 盘式制动　＿＿＿＿＿＿ brake

(11)分离轴承　release _____

(12)离合器片　clutch _____

(13)变速器控制模块　transmission control _____

 Game Time(游戏时间)

根据横向和纵向的图片圈出网格里相应汽车零部件的英文名称。

横向：

纵向：

c	v	t	d	i	s	c	a	i	p	f
s	p	r	i	n	g	z	s	r	k	j
u	t	a	f	e	b	a	c	r	l	w
s	a	n	f	n	s	b	c	s	m	a
p	j	s	e	u	o	s	h	a	f	t
e	h	m	r	p	b	o	b	e	r	r
n	i	i	e	z	u	r	q	v	a	s
s	w	s	n	t	p	b	v	c	m	q
i	p	s	t	y	r	e	w	i	e	p
o	d	i	i	w	r	r	o	e	r	o
n	w	o	a	g	c	l	u	t	c	h
m	d	n	l	e	w	w	t	p	e	w

3.2 Dismantle and Assemble Manual Transmission Input Shaft

（拆卸和安装手动变速器输入轴）

1. An Overview of a Manual Transmission

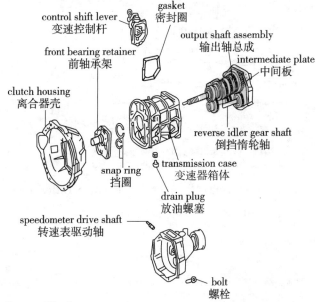

2. Dismantle Input Shaft

（1）For the next step, the end of the input shaft with the clutch plate splines must be placed in clamping device(T10306) and clamped in a vice.

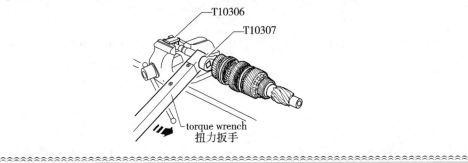

> **NOTICE：**
> The twelve-point nut has a "left-hand thread" (turn tool clockwise to unfasten nut).

(2) Unfasten twelve-point nut.

(3) Remove 4th speed selector gear with needle bearing and synchro-rings.

(4) Press off 3rd speed, 5th speed and 6th speed selector gears together with synchronising hub and needle bearing inner races.

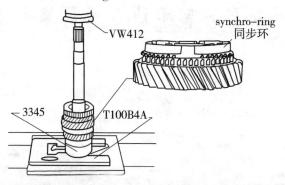

> **NOTICE:**
>
> It may be necessary to exert a pressure of up to 200 kN.

(5) Position bearing mounting(A) over input shaft roller bearing to prevent the rollers from being pressed out of the bearing cage.

(6) Press roller bearing off input shaft.

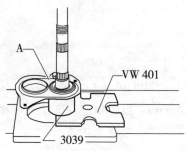

(7) Clean thread for twelve-point nut on input shaft to remove any residue of locking fluid.

3. Assemble Input Shaft

> **NOTICE:**
>
> Clean the input shaft thread.
>
> Lubricate all needle bearings and synchro-rings with gear oil before fitting.

(1) Heat needle bearing inner races to 130℃(max) before pressing on (wear

protective gloves).

(2) Heat synchronising hubs to 100℃ (max) before pressing on (wear protective gloves).

(3) Always press on roller bearing, needle bearing inner races and synchronising hubs as far as stop to make sure the axial clearance of the selector gears meets the specification.

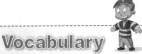

New Words(生词)

gasket	密封垫
circlip	卡环
nut	螺母
spanner	扳手
spline	花键
vice	台钳
hub	毂,轮毂
mounting	支架,装配
roller	滚子
specification	技术参数
assemble	装配,组合,组装
lubricate	润滑

Phrases(词组)

transmissions input shaft	变速器输入轴
control shift lever	变速控制杆
output shaft assembly	输出轴总成
front bearing retainer	前轴承架

reverse idler gear shaft	倒挡惰轮轴
ring gear housing	驱动桥壳
axle shaft	半轴
pinion gear	行星齿轮
drive pinion	主动小齿轮
thrust washer	止推垫片
side gear	半轴齿轮
snap ring	挡圈
drain plug	放油螺塞
speedometer drive shaft	转速表驱动轴
clamping device	夹紧装置
torque wrench	扭力扳手
selector gear	换挡齿轮
needle bearing	滚针轴承
locking fluid	防松剂
axial clearance	轴向间隙
synchro-ring	同步环

Exercises(练习)

1. 根据课文内容,请重新编排装配输入轴总成的工作顺序。

①将滚针轴承的内圈加热到最高 130℃,压入滚针轴承;②将同步器花键毂加热到 100℃,压入同步器花键毂;③在所有滚针轴承和同步环上涂齿轮油。

2. 根据课文内容,回答以下问题。

(1)图中编号 T10306、T10307 是指什么专用工具?

(2)安装同步体(synchronising hub)时应该如何处理,为什么?

3. 英译汉。

(1) Heat needle bearing inner races to 130℃ (max) before pressing on (wear protective gloves).

_____。

(2) Heat synchronising hubs to 100℃ (max) before pressing on (wear protective gloves).

_____。

 Game Time(游戏时间)

学生抽取一张写有手动变速器零部件英文单词的纸片,然后用中文描述这个零部件的功能、特点和它所在的位置,其他同学猜是哪个单词,如果哪位猜着,就用英文说出该单词。

3.3 General Notes of AT Component Parts Removal
（拆装自动变速器的注意事项）

1. Schematic View of Automatic Transmission

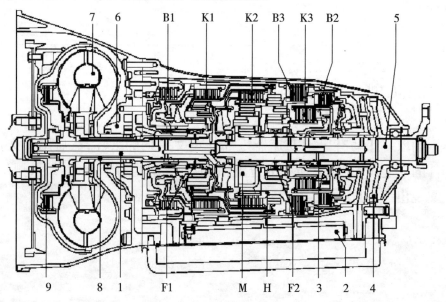

编号	英文	中文	编号	英文	中文
1	Drive shaft	驱动轴	B2	Rear multiple-disc brake	后多片式制动器
2	Electrohydraulic control unit	电液控制单元	B3	Center multiple-disc brake	中央多片式制动器
3	Intermediate shaft	中间轴	F1	Front freewheel	前自由轮
4	Parking lock gear	驻车锁止齿轮	F2	Rear freewheel	后自由轮
5	Output shaft	输出轴	H	Rear planetary gear set	后行星齿轮组
6	Oil pump	机油泵	K1	Front multiple-disc clutch	前多片式离合器
7	Torque converter	液力变扭器	K2	Center multiple-disc clutch	中央多片式离合器
8	Stator shaft	导轮轴	K3	Rear multiple-disc clutch	后多片式离合器
9	Torque converter lockup clutch	液力变扭器锁止离合器	M	Middle planetary gear set	中间行星齿轮组
B1	Front multiple-disc brake	前多片式制动器			

2. The Structure of a Torgue Converter

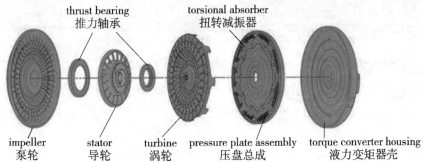

The instructions here are organized so that you work on only one component group at a time.

This will help avoid confusion from similar-looking parts of different subassemblies being on you workbench at the same time. The component groups are inspected and repaired from the converter housing side.

As much as possible, complete the inspection, repair and assembly before proceeding to the next component group. If a component group can not be assembled because parts are being ordered, be sure to keep all parts off that group in a separate container.

Use only recommended fluid for the automatic transmission.

3. General Cleaning Notes

(1) All disassembled parts should be washed clean and any fluid passages and holes blown through with compressed air.

(2) When using compressed air to dry parts, always aim away from yourself to prevent accidentally spraying automatic transmission fluid or kerosene in your face.

(3) The recommended automatic transmission fluid or kerosene should be used for cleaning.

4. Parts Arrangement

(1) After cleaning, the parts should be arranged in the correct order to allow efficient inspection, repairs, and reassembly.

(2) When disassembling a valve body, be sure to keep each valve together with the corresponding spring.

(3) New brakes and clutches that are to be used for replacement must be soaked in transmission fluid for at least fifteen minutes before assembly.

5. General Assembly

(1) All oil seal rings, clutch discs, clutch plates, rotating parts, and sliding surfaces should be coated with transmission fluid prior to reassembly.

(2) All gaskets and rubber O-rings should be replaced.

(3) Check thrust bearing and races for wear of damage. Replace if necessary.

(4) Use grease to keep parts in place.

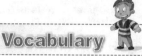

New Words(生词)

electrohydraulic	电液的
impeller	泵轮
stator	导轮
turbine	涡轮

Phrases(词组)

torque converter	液力变矩器
torque converter housing	液力变矩器壳
transmission control module	换挡控制模块
solenoid valve	电磁阀
dual planet carrier	双重行星齿轮托架
ring gear	齿圈
multiple-disc brake	多片式制动器
multiple-disc clutch	多片式离合器
planet gear	行星齿轮

Exercises(练习)

1. 翻译短文

As much as possible, complete the inspection, repair and assembly before proceeding to the next component group. If a component group can not be assembled because parts are being ordered, be sure to keep all parts off that group in a separate container.

_____

_____ 。

2. 根据课文内容判断下列描述是否正确

(1) All parts should be cleaned with compressed air.　　　　　(　　)

(2) Don't point the compressed air towards anybody.　　　　　(　　)

(3) When work on a valve body, put each valve and its washer together.

(　　)

(4) All new parts that will be installed must be soaked in transmission fluid for at least 15 minutes.　　　　　(　　)

(5) All gaskets and rubber O-rings are used only one time.　　　　　(　　)

3. 请选择正确的答案连线

(1) Impeller　　　　　　　　　　a. 涡轮
(2) Stator　　　　　　　　　　　b. 多片式制动器
(3) Turbine　　　　　　　　　　c. 多片式离合器
(4) Solenoid valve　　　　　　　d. 泵轮
(5) Ring gear　　　　　　　　　e. 行星齿轮
(6) Multiple-disc brake　　　　　f. 齿圈
(7) Multiple-disc clutch　　　　　g. 电磁阀
(8) Planetary gear　　　　　　　h. 导轮

Game Time(游戏时间)

教师在屏幕上投影出自动变速器的结构彩图,然后将学生分成若干小组,每组学生将写有自动变速器零件名称的卡片贴在彩图的相应位置上,正确完成任务且用时最短的小组胜出。

3.4 Install Front Axle Assembly
(装配前桥总成)

1. Parts Location

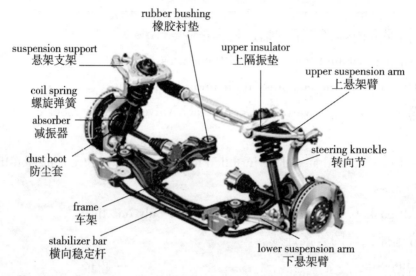

2. Installation

(1) Install front axle assembly.

a. Install the front axle assembly onto the shock absorber.

b. Install the 2 bolts and 2 nuts.

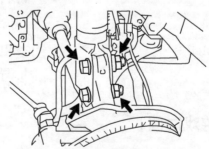

Torque: 164 N·m.

NOTICE:

Do not push the front axle further out of the vehicle than is necessary.

Do not damage the outboard joint boot.

Do not damage the speed sensor rotor.

（2）Install front lower suspension arm.

（3）Install front stabilizer link assembly.

（4）Install tie rod end sub-assembly.

（5）Install front disc.

（6）Install front disc brake caliper.

Install the disc brake caliper onto the steering knuckle.

Torque：107 N·m.

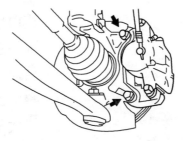

（7）Install front speed sensor.

（8）Install front axle hub nut.

（9）Install front axle hub bearing.

（10）Install front wheel.

Torque：103 N·m.

（11）Inspect and adjust front wheel alignment.

（12）Connect cable to negative battery terminal.

Torque：5.4 N·m.

（13）Check ABS sensor signal.

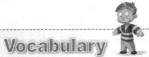

New Words（生词）

rotor	转子,转轮
sub-assembly	部件
frame	车架

Phrases(词组)

rubber bushing	橡胶衬垫
suspension support	悬架支架
upper insulator	上隔振垫
upper suspension arm	上悬架臂
stabilizer bar	横向稳定杆
front axle assembly	前桥总成
tie rod end	转向横拉杆球铰接头
stabilizer link assembly	稳定器固定柱
disc brake caliper	盘式制动卡钳
wheel alignment	车轮定位
sensor signal	传感器信号
control valve	控制阀
steering wheel	转向盘
steering knuckle	转向节
steering shaft	转向轴
steering gear(rack & pinion type)	转向器(齿轮齿条式)
power steering pump	动力转向泵
steering tie rod	转向横拉杆
oil reservoir	储油罐

 Exercises(练习)

1. 根据课文内容,请重新编排装配前桥总成的工作顺序

(1)安装安装前桥下悬架臂;(2)安装前横向稳定杆连接杆总成;(3)安装转向横拉杆末端分总成;(4)安装轮毂轴承;(5)安装前轮。扭矩103N·m;(6)检查和调整前轮定位;(7)将蓄电池负极接好;(8)检查 ABS 传感器;(9)安装前制动盘;(10)将前轮制动卡钳到转向节上。扭矩107N·m;(11)安装前轮速传感器;(12)安装前轴固定螺栓;(13)安装前轴总成。

正确的顺序是：

_____

2.根据课文内容,回答以下问题。

(1)拆卸前轴总成时应该注意哪些事项?

_____

(2)制动钳与转向节安装螺栓拧紧力矩是_____ N·m。
前轮安装螺栓拧紧力矩是拧紧力矩是_____ N·m。
蓄电池负极螺栓拧紧力矩是_____ N·m。

 Game Time(游戏时间)

请使用下列字母拼写相应的底盘专业词汇,每使用一个字母得一分,每个字母限用一次,相同的字母可使用的最多次数按该字母的给定次数,如字母 a 可最多可使用两次,字母 i 可最多可使用三次等。得分最多的同学即胜出。

a a b c d e e f g h i i i k l m n n o o o r s t t u y

例:nut 共使用3个字母,得3分。

3.5 Remove and Install Power Steering Gear Box
（拆卸和安装助力转向器）

1. Parts Location

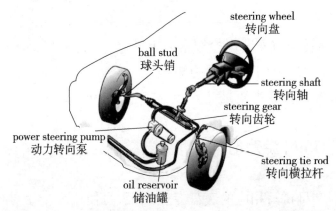

2. Remove Power Steering Gear Box

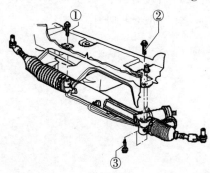

（1）Loosen bolt ① one turn.

（2）Remove bolts ② and ③.

（3）Pivot steering box forwards in direction of travel on driver's side.

（4）Place a drip tray underneath to catch hydraulic fluid.

（5）Use 22mm open-end ring spanner to unscrew banjo bolt (22mm) for return hose from steering gear box.

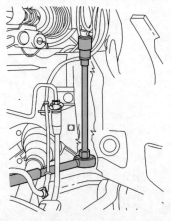

（6）Use 19mm open-end ring spanner to unscrew banjo bolt (19mm) for pressure hose from steering gear box.

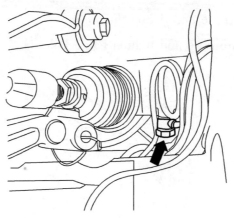

(7) Remove bolt ①.

(8) Take out steering box through left-hand wheel housing. (2nd mechanic required)

3. Installation

(1) Before installing, centralise steering box using steering centring bolt(VAS 6224).

(2) Remove hexagon socket head bolt 1 on steering box.

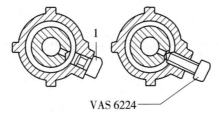

(3) Move steering rack until centre marking (indentation) on rack (arrow) aligns with threaded hole 2.

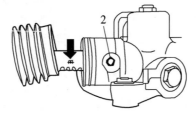

(4) Screw in steering centring bolt(VAS 6224) hand-tight.

(5) Position steering box (2nd mechanic required). Make sure threads and contact surfaces of bolts are free from oil and grease.

(6) Insert bolt ① but do not tighten.

（7）Pivot steering box forwards in direction of travel on driver's side.

（8）Connect return hose and tighten banjo bolt ②.

（9）Connect pressure hose and tighten banjo bolt ①.

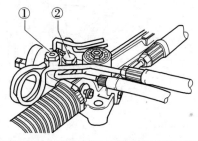

NOTICE：

Always use new seals for banjo bolts.

Pressure hose and return hose must not touch each other or come into contact with other parts.

（10）Insert bolt ② but do not tighten.

（11）Install and tighten bolt ③.

（12）Tighten bolts ① and ②.

（13）Release steering lock.

（14）Set steering wheel to centre position and then attach universal joint to steering pinion.

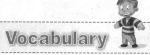

Vocabulary

 New Words（生词）

bulkhead	隔板
rack	齿条
seal	密封件

 Phrases（词组）

banjo bolt   带孔螺栓

hexagon socket head bolt　　　内六角螺栓
universal joint　　　万向接头

Exercises(练习)

1. 根据课文内容,请重新编排安装助力转向器的工作顺序

(1)将拆下的转向器用转向中心定位螺栓(VAS 6224)固定;(2)为此应旋出转向器上的内六角螺栓 1;(3)推移齿条,直至齿条上的定心件(按箭头方向)对准螺纹孔 2;(4)用手拧入转向中心定位螺栓(VAS 6224);(5)对排水槽上的转向器定位(需要第二位机械师帮助);(6)安装螺栓①,但不要拧紧;(7)把驾驶员侧的转向器沿行驶方向向前翻转;(8)连接回流软管并把 22 mm 带孔螺栓 2 拧紧;(9)连接压力软管并把 19mm 带孔螺栓 1 拧紧;(10)安装螺栓②,但不要拧紧;(11)装入螺栓 ③ 并拧紧;(12)现在可以拧紧螺栓① 和 ②;(13)转向锁开锁;(14)将转向盘打到中间位置,然后将十字接头插入转向小齿轮。

正确的顺序是:

_____

_____

2. 根据课文内容,回答以下问题

(1)松开转向液软管螺母前需要放置什么?

_____

(2)如何将助力转向器从车底下移出,需要几个技师?

_____

(3)22mm 带孔螺母装在哪条软管上,19mm 带孔螺母装在哪条软管上?

_____

3. 翻译句子

(1)Use 22mm open-end ring spanner to unscrew banjo bolt (19 mm) for pressure hose from steering gear box.

_____

（2）Remove hexagon socket head bolt 1 on steering box. Move steering rack until centre marking (indentation) on rack (arrow) aligns with threaded hole 2.

（3）Always use new seals for banjo bolts.

（4）Pressure hose and return hose must not touch each other or come into contact with other parts.

Game Time（游戏时间）

填字游戏：

在下列空格中填入相应的字母，使得横向、纵向分别构成相应的单词。

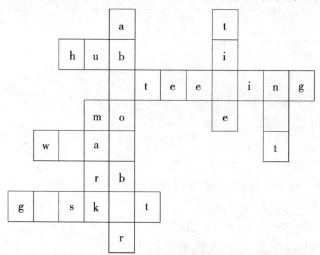

Chapter 3 Automobile Chassis

3.6 Remove and Install Brake Pads
（拆卸和安装制动摩擦片）

1. Parts Location

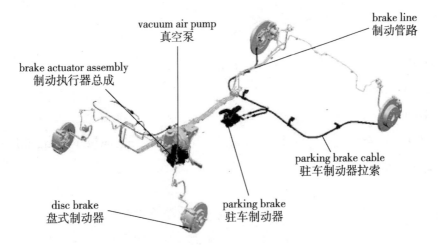

2. The Structure of Disc Brake

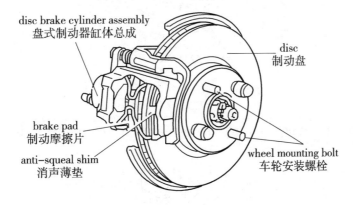

3. Removal

NOTICE：

Mark brake pads when removing them if they are to be reinstalled. Reinstall in their original position to prevent uneven braking.

（1）On vehicles equipped with a brake pad wear indicator, unplug connector 1.

(2) Slightly lift up locating lug on lower part of connector 2 and turn 90°.

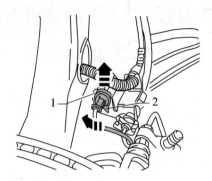

(3) Pull lower half of connector out of bracket.

(4) Raise vehicle.

(5) Remove wheels.

(6) Remove securing bolts from brake caliper housing, when doing this counter-hold on guide pins.

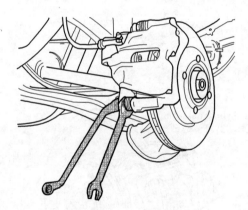

(7) Fold brake caliper housing upwards and take out brake pads.

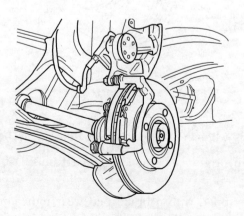

(8) Press piston back.

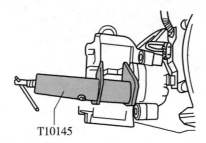

NOTICE:

Before inserting new brake pads, press piston back into cylinder with resetting appliance.

Before pressing the piston back, draw off brake fluid from the reservoir with a bleeder bottle.

Otherwise, fluid can overflow and cause damage, particularly if reservoir has been topped up.

WARNING:

Brake fluid is poisonous and must NOT be sucked through a hose with the mouth.

(9) Fit brake pads.
(10) Fold brake caliper housing down and tighten securing bolt to 30 N·m.

NOTICE:

After each brake pad change firmly depress brake pedal several times with vehicle stationary, so that the brake pads are properly seated in their normal operating position.

(11) Install wheels.
(12) Check brake fluid level and top up if necessary.

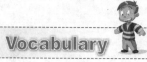

 New Words(生词)

wear	磨损
indicator	指示器
unplug	拔去(电源)插头
connector	连接器,连接插头
reservoir	储液罐

 Phrases(词组)

disc brake	盘式制动器
disc brake cylinder assembly	盘式制动器缸体总成
brake pad	制动摩擦片
wheel mounting bolt	车轮安装螺栓
anti-squeal shim	消声薄垫
vacuum air pump	真空泵
brake actuator assembly	制动执行器总成
parking brake cable	驻车制动器拉索
securing bolt	锁紧螺栓
locating lug	定位销
bracket	托架,支架
guide pin	导向销
resetting appliance	复位工具
brake fluid	制动液

 Exercises(练习)

1. 根据课文内容,请重新编排拆卸制动摩擦片步骤的工作顺序

(1)升起汽车;(2)拆下车轮;(3)固定住导向销,从制动钳体上拧下固定螺钉;(4)对于有制动摩擦片磨损显示器的汽车,脱开插头连接1;(5)将插头下部上的固定凸耳2略微抬起,并随后转动90°;(6)将插头下部件从支架上拔出;(7)将制动钳体向上翻转,并取出制动摩擦片;(8)复位活塞;(9)将制动钳体向下翻转,并以30N·m拧紧紧固螺栓;(10)装入制动摩擦片;(11)安装车轮;(12)检查制动液液位,必要时添加。

正确的顺序是:

_____

2. 根据课文内容,回答以下问题

(1)拆卸前为什么要在继续使用的制动摩擦片上做好记号?

_____

(2)用什么工具抽出制动液?

_____

3. 翻译短文

After each brake pad change firmly depress brake pedal several times with vehicle stationary, so that the brake pads are properly seated in their normal operating position.

_____

Reading Material(阅读材料)

Introduction of New Models

Conversation 1	**对话1**
Salesman: Now I'd like to show you the new model, Toyota Landcruiser.	销售员:现在我向您介绍一款新车,丰田陆地巡洋舰。
Customer: Oh, it looks nice.	顾 客:很漂亮。
Salesman: Yes, I bet you'll like it more after my introduction. It's power steering with alloy wheels, cruise control, and 4 wheel drive.	销售员:我肯定在听完我的介绍之后您会更喜欢它。它带动力转向的合金车轮,有巡航系统和四轮驱动。

Customer: Very good. Could you tell me more about the specifications of this model?

Salesman: Sure. As you can see it's of sports utility body style with mahogany exterior, 4.7 Liter V8 engine.

Customer: I like it very much. What's the price?

Salesman: $ 49975.00.

Customer: Any discount?

Salesman: Yes, We can offer you 5% off.

Customer: Good. I'll take it.

Conversation 2

Salesman: This way, Mr. Smith. What do you think about our new model Audi A6 Quattro?

Customer: Oh, it looks good. But I'd like to know something about its feature.

Salesman: It's auto transmission and 4 wheel drive with power brakes. Let me tell you more specification. The Mileage is 14,415. The engine, 4.2 Liter V6. The price is $ 27299.00. I think it's quite a good car.

Customer: Yes, I think so. But I'd like to look around and make a decision after seeing some other models.

Salesman: Sure.

顾　客：很好。你能告诉我关于这款车更多的特点吗？

销售员：当然。它的发动机是4.7L V8发动机。正如您所见，这辆车有红褐色运动型的外壳，非常好看。

顾　客：我非常喜欢。它的售价是多少呢？

销售员：49975.00 美元。

顾　客：打折吗？

销售员：可以，我们可以给您便宜5%。

顾　客：好的，那我就买吧。

对话2

销售员：请这边，史密斯先生。你觉得我们的新款奥迪 A6 Quattro 如何？

顾　客：看上去不错。但是我想多了解一些它的特性。

销售员：这辆车装备有自动变速器和带有动力制动的四轮驱动系统。让我告诉你更多它的特性：这辆车行驶了14415 英里，4.2L V6 发动机，售价是27299 美元。我觉得这是一辆很好的车。

顾　客：是的，我也这么想。但我还是想再看看其他的型号的车然后决定。

销售员：好的。

Chapter 3　Automobile Chassis

Conversation 3

Salesman: Are you interested in our new model? Would you like to know more about it?

Customer: Yes, I would. But does it have Anti-Lock Brakes and Auto Transmission?

Salesman: Yes, of course. And also with the other features such as Dual Air Bags, Tilt Wheel and Power Locks Etc.

Customer: Perfect. I love it. I think I'll take this one.

Salesman: Thank you.

对话 3

销售员：你对我们这款新车有兴趣吗？要多了解一下吗？

顾　客：好的。它有防抱死制动系统和自动变速器吗？

销售员：当然有。而且还有其他的特性，如双气囊、可调式转向盘和电动门锁等。

顾　客：太好了，我很喜欢。我想买这辆。

销售员：谢谢。

3.7　Wheel Alignment(车轮定位)

1. Inspect Tires
2. Measure Vehicle Height

NOTICE:

Before inspecting the wheel alignment, adjust the vehicle height to the specified value.

Be sure to perform measurement on a level surface.

If it is necessary to go under the vehicle for measurement, confirm that the parking brake is applied and the vehicle is secured with chocks.

(1)Bounce the vehicle up and down at the corners several times to stabilize the suspension.

(2)Measure the vehicle height.

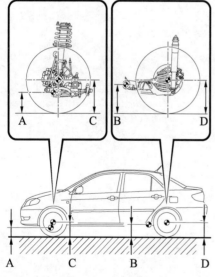

Measuring points:

A	No. 1 lower suspension arm bushing set bolt ground clearance
B	Rear axle beam set bolt ground clearance
C	Front wheel center ground clearance
D	Rear wheel center ground clearance

Vehicle Height (Unloaded Vehicle):

Engine	Front C-A	Rear D-B
2ZR-FE	92mm	45mm

3. Inspect Wheel Angle.

(1)Put tread center marks on the rearmost points of the turning radius gauge.

(2)Turn the steering wheel to the left and right full lock positions, and measure the turning angle.

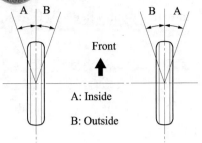

Wheel Angle (Unloaded Vehicle):

Engine	Tire Size	Inside Wheel	Outside Wheel Reference
2ZR-FE	195/65R15	38°13′ ±2°	38°50′
	205/55R16		

A: Inside
B: Outside

If the angles are not as specified, check and adjust the right and left rack end lengths.

4. Inspect Camber, Caster and Steering Axis Inclination

(1) Install a camber-caster-kingpin gauge or place the front wheels on the center of a wheel alignment tester.

(2) Inspect the camber, caster and steering axis inclination.

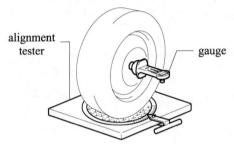

Camber (Unloaded Vehicle):

Engine	Tire Size	Camber Inclination	Right-Left Difference
2ZR-FE	195/65R15	−0°35′	45′ or less
	205/55R16	±45′	

5. Adjust Camber

6. Inspect Toe-In

(1) Bounce the vehicle up and down at the corners several times to stabilize the suspension.

(2) Release the parking brake and move the shift lever to N.

(3) Push the vehicle straight ahead approximately 5 m. (*1)

(4) Put tread center marks on the rearmost points of the front wheels and measure the distance between the marks (dimension B).

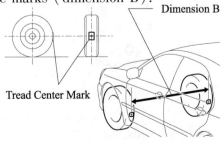

(5) Slowly push the vehicle straight ahead to rotate the front wheels 180° using the front tire valve as a reference point.

> **NOTICE:**
> Do not allow the wheels to rotate more than 180°. If the wheels rotate more than 180°, perform the procedure from (*1) again.

(6) Measure the distance between the tread center marks on the front side of the wheels (dimension A).

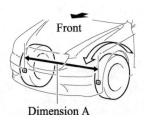

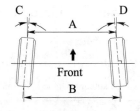

Toe-in:

Specified Condition
C + D: 0°00′ ± −0°12′
B - A: 0 ± 2.0mm

> **NOTICE:**
> Measure "B − A" only when "C + D" cannot be measured.
> If the toe-in is not within the specified range, adjust it at the rack ends.

7. Adjust Toe-In

(1) Make sure that the lengths of the right and left rack ends are almost the same.

Difference between right and left rack ends: 1.5 mm or less.

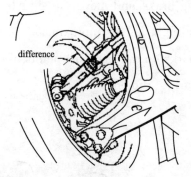

(2) Remove the boot clips.

(3) Loosen the tie rod end lock nuts.

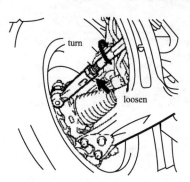

(4) Turn the right and left rack ends by an equal amount to adjust the toe-in to the center value.

①Extend the shorter rack end if the measured toe-in deviates toward the outer side.

②Shorten the longer rack end if the measured toe-in deviates toward the inner side.

(5) Tighten the tie rod end lock nuts.

Torque: 74 N·m.

(6) Place the boots on the seats and install the clips.

NOTICE:
Make sure that the boots are not twisted.

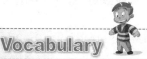

New Words(生词)

camber	外倾角
caster	后倾角
kingpin	主销

Phrases(词组)

toe-in	前束

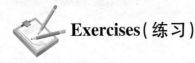 **Exercises**(练习)

1. 根据课文内容,回答以下问题

(1)补充检查车辆前束的步骤:
①反复按压车辆数次使悬架稳定;②释放驻车制动器,将换挡杆推入 N 挡;

(2)调整车辆前束时有哪些注意事项?

2. 翻译短文

If it is necessary to go under the vehicle for measurement, confirm that the parking brake is applied and the vehicle is secured with chocks.

Extend Reading(拓展阅读)

Wheel Alignment

Wheel alignment, sometimes referred to as breaking or tracking, is part of standard automobile maintenance that consists of adjusting the angles of wheels so that they are set to the car maker's specification. The purpose of these adjustments is to reduce tire wear, and to ensure that vehicle travel is straight and true (without "pulling" to one side).

All new vehicles leave the factory with their alignment checked and adjusted. It is advisable to do the alignment of the car after the first 5000 km, since all the suspension get set. Failure to do this may result in the camber and toe specifications drifting outside the manufacturer's limit. This may lead to vehicle pulling and tire wear. Tire wear leads to frequent replacement of tires thus adding to running cost for the consumer. Vehicle pulling causes irritation and/or fatigue while driving the car.

Chapter 4 Automobile Electric
（汽车电器）

4.1 The General Introduction of the Auto Electrical System
（汽车电气系统的总体介绍）

1. An Overview of the Auto Electrical System

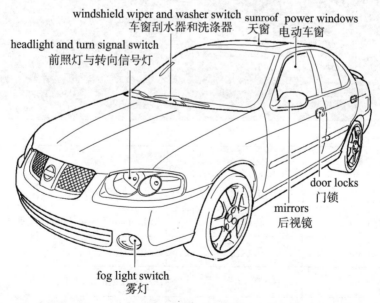

With the development of the vehicle, more and more electrical equipments (besides the traditional electrical equipments) have been used in the vehicle to improve its comfort and safety.

2. The Lighting System

The lighting system is consist of the headlamp, the fog lamp, the tail lamp and the license plate light.

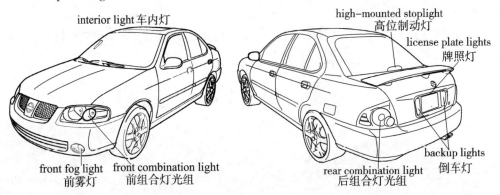

3. The Combination Meter

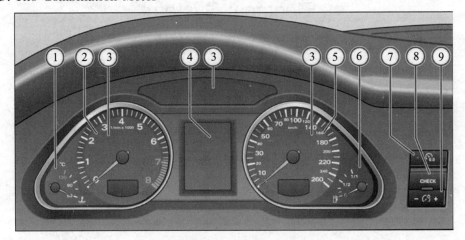

编号	英文	中文	编号	英文	中文
1	Water temperature gauge	水温表	6	Fuel gauge	燃油表
2	Tachometer	转速表	7	"trip meter" reset button	短距离里程表复位按钮
3	Indicator	指示器	8	"CHECK" button	发动机故障灯按钮
4	Monitor	显示屏	9	Display bright/dark button	亮度调节按钮
5	Speedometer	车速表			

4. The Charging System

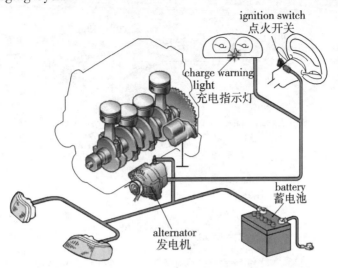

5. The Starting System

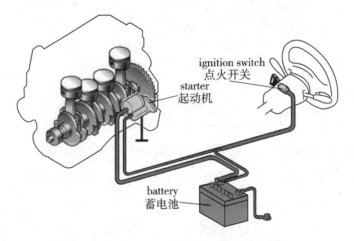

6. The Wiper and Washer System

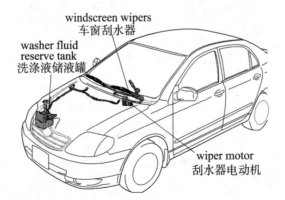

7. The Air Conditioning System

The air conditioning system is consist of the heater system and the cooling system.

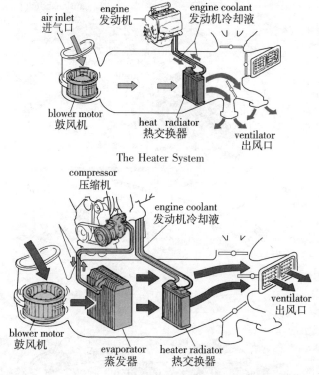

The Heater System

The Cooling System

8. The Supplemental Electrical System

The supplemental electrical system is consist of the supplemental restraint system, the power door lock control system and so on. With the use of the supplemental electrical system, comfort and safety of a vehicle can be improved.

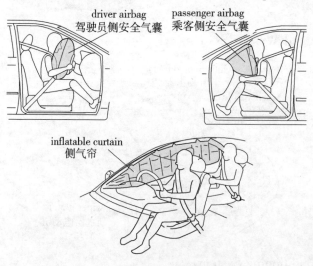

The Supplemental Restraint System

Chapter 4 Automobile Electric

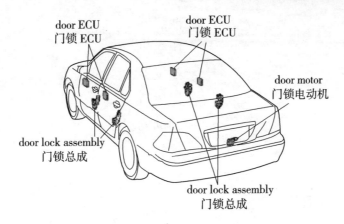

The Power Door Lock Control System

Vocabulary

New Words(生词)

electrical	电气的
equipment	设备
headlight	前照灯
lamp	灯
interior	内部的
light	灯
combination	组合
gauge	计量器
monitor	显示屏
tachometer	转速表
speedometer	车速表
display	显示
alternator	发电机
starter	起动机
wiper	刮水器
washer	洗涤器

radiator	散热器
compressor	压缩机
evaporator	蒸发器
ventilator	出风口
supplemental	辅助的
airbag	气囊

 Phrases(词组)

lighting system	照明系统
wiper and washer system	刮水和清洗系统
charging system	充电系统
combination meter	组合仪表
trip meter	短距离里程表
fog light	雾灯
stop light	制动灯
back-up light	倒车灯
license plate light	牌照灯
air conditioning system	空调系统
heater system	加热系统
cooling system	制冷系统
supplemental restraint system	辅助约束系统
power door lock control system	电动门锁控制系统
inflatable curtain	侧气帘

 Exercises(练习)

1. 根据课文内容,完成下列填空

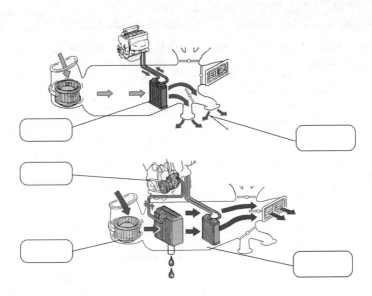

2. 给下面的示意图标记

	A.
	B.
	C.
	D.

3. 根据功能描述找出相对应的部件名称

| battery combination meter turn signal lights alternator ESP EPS EPC |

功　能	部　件　名　称
当发电机不工作时,该设备用作备用电源	
除了蓄电池外,汽车的第二个电源	
防止汽车侧滑的系统	
车辆变道或转向时需要操作的设备	
使用电动机作为转向助力的系统	

Chapter 4 Automobile Electric

4.2 How to Use Electrical Equipments
（如何使用电器设备）

1. An Overview of the Center Console

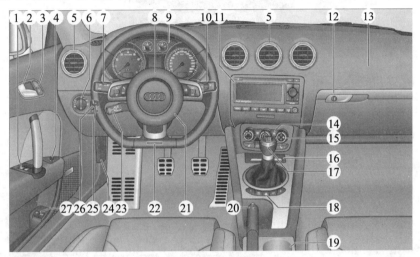

编号	英文	中文	编号	英文	中文
1	Electric windows	电动车窗	15	Air conditioner	空调
2	Door handle	车门抠手	16	Ashtray, cigarette lighter/socket	烟灰缸，点烟器/插座
3	Central locking switch	中控锁开关	17	Gear lever	变速杆
4	Electric adjuster for exterior mirrors	外后视镜调节器	18	ESP	电控车辆稳定行驶系统
5	Air outlets	出风口	19	Cup holder	杯架
6	Light switch	灯开关	20	Handbrake	驻车制动器操纵杆
7	Lever for turn signals and main beam headlight	转向灯及车灯主控制杆	21	Ignition lock	点火锁
8	Controls near the steering wheel	转向盘附近控制器	22	Adjustable steering column	可调转向柱
9	Instrument cluster	组合仪表	23	Lever for cruise control	巡航控制杆
10	Windscreen wiper and washer	风窗玻璃刮水器和洗涤器	24	Bonnet lock release	发动机舱盖开启拉手
11	Radio or navigation system	收音机或导航系统	25	Headlight range control	前照灯范围控制
12	Lockable glove box	可锁手套箱	26	Instrument lighting	仪表灯
13	Front passenger's airbag	前排乘员气囊	27	Switches for unlocking the tailgate	行李舱盖开启开关
14	Switch for heated rear window	后窗加热开关			

2. Headlights

Switching on the dipped lights

- Turn the light switch to position ≣D.

Switching off the lights

- Turn the light switch to position O.

The dipped beam headlights will only work with the ignition on.

NOTICE:

If the lights are left on after the key has been taken out of the ignition lock, a buzzer sounds when the driver's door is opened.

If you set the switch to "AUTO", the headlights will come on and switch off automatically according to the ambient light level.

Activating automatic headlights

- Turn the light switch to the AUTO position.

Deactivating automatic headlights

- Turn the light switch to position O.

NOTICE:

The automatic headlight setting only activates the dipped beam headlights (not the main beam headlights).

If a malfunction should occur in the light sensor, a symbol will light up in the display. For safety reasons, the dipped beam headlights will then be switched on permanently when the light switch is set to the AUTO position.

Do not attach any stickers to the windscreen in front of the sensor, as this would interfere with the operation of the automatic headlights and the automatic anti-dazzle function for the mirrors.

3. Fog Lights

Front fog lights

- Do not turn the light switch to the symbol ≹O
- First turn the light switch to the position ≹O or ⊃∈. Then pull out the light switch to the first stop 1.

Rear fog light

- Do not turn the light switch to the symbol O≹.
- First turn the light switch to the position ⊃∈ or ≹O. Then pull out the light switch to the second stop 2 to switch on the rear fog light.

NOTICE:

The front fog light symbol ≹O next to the switch will light up when the front fog lights are on.

The symbols ≹O and O≹ next to the switch will light up when the rear fog light is switched on.

To avoid dazzling the traffic behind you, the rear fog light should only be used in accordance with statutory regulations.

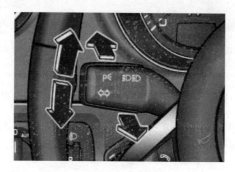

4. Turn Signals and Main Beam Headlights

Turn signals

– Move the lever all the way up to indicate right, or all the way down to indicate left.

– Move the lever up or down to the point of resistance and hold it there to signal briefly, for instance when changing lane.

Main beam headlights

– Press the lever forward to switch on the main beams.

– Pull the lever back towards you to switch the main beam headlights off again.

NOTICE:

The main beam headlights can only be switched on if the dipped beam headlights are already on.

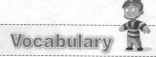

 New Words(生词)

compartment	车厢
handle	把手
navigation	导航
ashtray	烟灰缸
cruise	巡航
bonnet	给……装上罩
tailgate	后挡板

symbol	符号
buzzer	蜂鸣器
activate	激活
brief	暂时的
automatically	自动地
malfunction	故障,机能失常
windscreen	风窗玻璃
accordance	一致,符合
statutory	法令的,法治的

Phrases(词组)

electric windows	电动车窗
central locking	中央门锁
light switch	灯光开关
turn signal light	转向信号灯
instrument cluster	仪表板
switching off	关闭
switching on	打开

Exercises(练习)

1. 请选择正确的答案

(1) 在_____接通的情况下,远光灯才能点亮。

    A. daytime running lights   B. hazard warning lights

    C. dipped beam headlights   D. Parking lights

(2) 光线传感器安装在车上的_____位置。

    A. windscreen   B. headlight

    C. instrument cluster   D. Rear-view mirrors

(3) 灯光开关用_____符号表示。

    A.   B.   C.   D.

（4）在_____的情况下,近光灯才能工作。

　　A. the light switch to the AUTO position

　　B. the light switch to position O

　　C. the ignition on

　　D. the light switch to the position 彐D

2. 根据课文内容判断下列描述是否正确

（1）Front fog lights：Turn the light switch to the symbol 彐D.　　　　　　（　）

（2）The automatic headlight setting only activates the main beam headlights.

　　　　　　　　　　　　　　　　　　　　　　　　　　　　　　　　　　（　）

（3）To avoid dazzling the traffic behind you, the rear fog light should only be used in accordance with statutory regulations.　　　　　　　　　　　　（　）

（4）The main beam headlights can be switched on unless the dipped beam headlights are already on.　　　　　　　　　　　　　　　　　　　　　　　（　）

（5）The symbols 彐D and 0彐 next to the switch will light up when the rear fog light is switched on.　　　　　　　　　　　　　　　　　　　　　　　　　　（　）

3. 根据方框里面的词,完成下列内容

turn　pull　set　move　next to　press　attach　hold

（1）If you _____ the switch to "AUTO", the headlights will come on.

（2）_____ the lever all the way up to indicate right, or all the way down to indicate left.

（3）_____ the lever forward to switch on the main beams.

（4）The front fog light symbol 彐D _____ the switch will light up when the front fog lights are on.

（5）Do not _____ any stickers to the windscreen in front of the sensor.

（6）First move lever up or down to the point of resistance and _____ it there to signal briefly, for instance when changing lane.

（7）First _____ the light switch to the position 彐D or 彐ଽ.

（8）_____ the lever back towards you to switch the main beam headlights off again.

Chapter 4 Automobile Electric

4. 下面是奥迪某车型的部分配置表,阅读并回答下列问题

Legend	S4 Sedan(轿车)	S4 Avant(旅行车)
× = Standard O = Optional — = Not available		
Exterior Lighting		
Aerodynamic 2-way ellipsoid projector headlamp assembly with VF (variable focus) reflectors, integrated low beam and high beam tubes	×	×
Two front fog lights located in lower front bumper	×	×
One rear fog light in left rear light	×	×
Rear light assemblies with white side turn indicators and amber shine-through bulbs	×	×
Daytime running lights utilizing front fog lights (Canada only)	×	×
Xenon headlights with automatic self leveling	×	×
White side turn indicator lights in front fenders with amber shine-through bulbs	×	×
Comfort / Convenience		
Fully automatic dual-zone climate control system with seven temperature sensors, sun sensor and pressure sensor. Also includes active charcoal and electro-static filters, which sense pollen, odors, bacteria and dust	×	×
Smog sensor for air-conditioning which automatically shuts off outside air and starts air-recirculation when smog detected	×	×
Homelink® universal garage door opener in driver's sunvisor	O	O
Front and rear power windows with	×	×
Two stage button mechanism	—	—
Power retention feature, which keeps power for windows and sunroof on until either front door open	—	—
"Pinch protection" for all four windows which reverses window at force of 100 N or greater	—	—
"One-touch" up and down for front and rear windows at all window locations	—	—
Illuminated driver controlled lock out switch for rear power windows	—	—
Electronic cruise control (two-stage switch) with coast, resume, speed-up, controlled by a lever on left side of steering wheel; cruise control indicator located in the instrument panel	×	×
Auto-Blink feature enables turn signals to automatically blink three times when blinker lever briefly pushed up /down (common when changing lane)	×	×

（1）哪些国家的车型上配有白昼行车灯？

_____

（2）在上述配置表中，轿车和旅行车各有几个前雾灯，分别位于汽车的什么位置？

_____

（3）上述两种车型的定速巡航控制按钮位于什么位置？

_____

（4）上述配置表中，每个车型有几个后雾灯，分别位于什么位置？

_____

（5）上述表中"×"，"—"，"○"分别代表什么意思？

_____

 Game Time（游戏时间）

教师将学生分成若干小组，给每组派发5~10印有汽车符合的卡片，如印有 🔑 的卡片，各小组成员根据纸片的内容用英文写出相应的词汇，教师根据各组的完成情况决定优胜的小组。

Chapter 4　Automobile Electric

4.3　Check and Adjust Headlight Settings
（检查和调整前照灯设置）

1. An Overview of Headlight Alignment

Have you ever been blinded by someone else's headlights, or noticed that your own headlights are not illuminating the road directly in front of you? If all you can see is the foliage on the side of the road, or oncoming drivers are constantly flashing their high beams or honking the horn at you, something is amiss. People who replace their own headlights may not adjust the headlights correctly, or a car accident may cause a misalignment. Whatever the cause, the following steps will enlighten you about how to adjust headlights to stop blinding other drivers.

Incorrect Headlight Alignment(too High)

Incorrect Headlight Alignment(too Low)

Correct Headlight Alignment

2. Requirements for Checking and Adjusting

(1) Ensure that the tire pressure is OK.

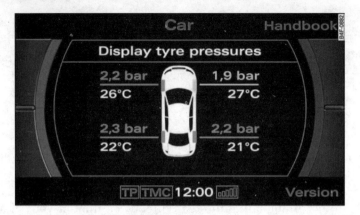

(2) Ensure that the reflectors and bulbs are OK.

> **NOTICE**:
> Lenses must not be damaged or dirty.

(3) Ensure that the vehicle is loaded correctly.

Loading: With one person or 75 kg on the driver's seat and the vehicle otherwise unloaded.

Read off fuel level in fuel tank on fuel gauge. Calculate additional weight according to the following table and place weight into boot.

Capacity table

Fuel Level on Fuel Gauge	Front-Wheel Drive Additional Weight in kg	Four-Wheel Drive Additional Weight in kg
1/4	55	60
1/2	35	40
3/4	20	20
full	0	0

(4) Ensure that the headlight adjuster is positioned 30 cm in front of the headlight.

Position headlight adjustment unit in front of headlight at distance a = 30cm. Dimension b = 3cm must not be exceeded (measured from headlight centre).

3. Checking Headlight Setting

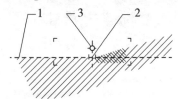

(1) The horizontal light-dark border should coincide with the setting line 1 of the test surface on the headlight adjustment unit.

(2) The break-away point 2 between the horizontal section of the light-dark border on the left and the rising section on the right should coincide with the vertical line running through the central point 3. The bright spot in the centre of the beam should be to the right of the vertical line.

4. Adjusting Headlights

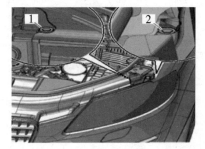

Adjuster screws on left headlight:

To adjust the height turn the adjuster screws 1 and 2 with the same number of turns.

To perform lateral adjustment only turn adjuster screw 2.

New Words(生词)

alignment	校正
illuminate	照明

flash	闪光
horn	喇叭
lenses	镜片
reflector	反射器
bulb	灯泡
boot	行李舱
horizontal	水平的
border	边界,边缘
spot	斑点,污点
screw	螺钉
load	负荷,载重

Phrases(词组)

fuel tank	油箱
tire pressure	胎压
front-wheel drive	前轮驱动
four-wheel drive	四轮驱动

Exercises(练习)

1. 将下图中的英文译成中文

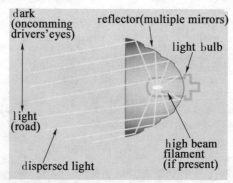

_____ _____ _____

_____ _____ _____

2. 根据课文内容回答问题

(1) 如果燃油箱只加注了容积的一半,在前轮驱动的车上必须在行李舱内放置多种附加配重?

_____。

(2) 在进行前照灯调整的过程中,都用到了哪些工具?

_____。

(3) 在进行前照灯调整之前,需要满足那些基本条件?

_____。

(4) 进行前照灯调整是对于仪器的摆放位置有没有什么要求?

_____。

3. 按照下面英文的带前照灯照明距离自动调节车辆的检查和调整步骤,将译文内容重新排序

(1) Before checking/adjusting headlights, always use the VAS 5051 to bring the headlights into their basic position.

(2) Performing basic setting using vehicle diagnostic, testing and information system VAS 5051.

(3) Connect vehicle diagnostic, testing and information system VAS 5051 using adapter cable VAS 5051/5. Ignition must be switched off.

(4) Switch on ignition.

(5) Select "Guided fault-finding", enter vehicle data, and then all control units will be interrogated.

(   ) 按压引导型故障查询:输入汽车数据,查询所有控制器。

(   ) 如要检查/调节前照灯,请务必用 VAS 5051 将它们置于基准位置。

(   ) 在点火开关关闭情况下将车辆诊断、测量和信息系统 VAS 5051 与适配导线 VAS 5051/5 连接。

(   ) 接通点火开关。

(   ) 用车辆诊断、测量和信息系统 VAS 5051 进行基本设置。

4. 阅读下面的材料,根据材料内容总结灯光线束偏离的原因

Headlights can become misaligned in many ways. One of the most common is when the person replacing a bad light inadvertently turns the adjusting screws instead of the retaining fasteners. Fender-benders and other front-end damage can also cause lights to become askew.

 Game Time(游戏时间)

　　五位学生在其他同学们面前站成一排。老师给第一位学生说一个灯光方面的词汇,该学生把这个词通过肢体动作传给第二位。该词就这样被小组同学依次悄悄地传递下去,最后这位学生可以把答案用英文或者中文告诉大家!

4.4 How to Read the Air Conditioning Wiring Diagram
（如何阅读空调电路图）

1. An Overview of an Air Conditioning

The air conditioning system delivers cooled air into the passenger compartment by circulating refrigerant through the system as follow: compressor → condenser → receiver/dryer → expansion valve → evaporator →compressor.

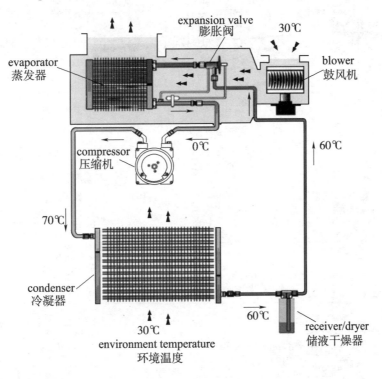

2. The Wiring Diagram of the Air Conditioning

The Air Conditioning Wiring System is consist of battery, radiator fan relay, ignition switch, radiator fan control module, condenser fan relay, compressor clutch relay, blower resistor, heater control panel, radiator fan motor and engine coolant temperature switch.

(1) Indicates the wiring color.

Wire colors are indicated by an alphabetical code.

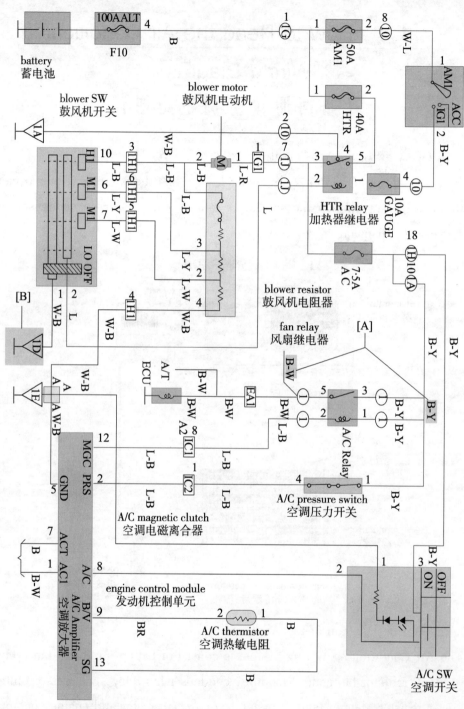

B-Black; W-White; BR-Brown; L-Blue; V-Violet; SB-Sky Blue; R-Red; G-Green; LG-Light Green; P-Pink; Y-Yellow; GR-Gray; O-Orange

Example: L - Y

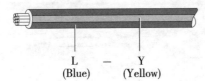

The first letter indicates the basic wire color and the second letter indicates the color of the stripe.

(2) Indicates the ground point.

The code consists of the two characters: A letter and a number.

Example:

The first character of the code indicates a serial number used to distinguish between the ground points in cases when more than one ground point exist on the same wire harness.

The second character indicates the alphabetical code allocated to the wire harness.

(3) Indicates the battery.

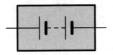

A battery stores chemical energy and converts it into electrical energy to provide DC current for the various electrical circuits of the auto.

(4) Indicate fuses.

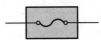

Fuses used in the wiring diagram of air conditioning are showed in table below.

Fuses	熔断丝
ALT 100A	ALT 100A
AM1 50A	AM1 50A
HTR 40A	加热器 40A
AC 7.5A	空调 7.5A
GAUGE 10A	仪表 10A

(5) Indicates the ignition switch.

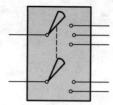

The ignition switch is a key operated switch with several positions.

(6) Indicates the relay.

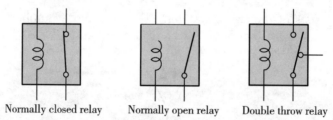

Normally closed relay　　Normally open relay　　Double throw relay

Basically, a relay is an electrically operated switch which may be normally closed or open. Current flow through a small coil creates a magnetic field which either opens or closes an attached switch.

Double throw relay is a relay which passes current through one set of contacts or the other.

(7) Indicates the blower resister.

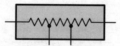

The blower resister is a tapped resistor which supplies two or more different non adjustable resistance values.

(8) Indicates the pressure switch.

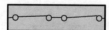

The purpose of the pressure switch determines whether it opens or closes on a rise or fall in pressure.

(9) Indicates the thermistor.

The thermistor is a resistor which varies its resistance with temperature.

(10) Indicates the connection position of a wire.

Example: 18 ①H

The number "1" in the circle is the J/B (Junction Block) number, and the connector code "H" is shown beside it. The number "18" is the 18 terminal of the connector H.

3. Air Conditioner Operation

When the blower switch is set on, the current flows from the HTR fuse to the HTR relay to the A/C fuse to the terminal 3 of the A/C switch. If the A/C switch is turned on, at this time a signal is input into the engine control module. This activates the engine control module and M/G CLT relay. So that current flows from the A/C fuse to M/G CLT relay to A/C magnetic clutch.

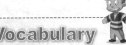

New Words(生词)

refrigerant	制冷剂
condenser	冷凝器
fan	风扇
resistor	电阻器
relay	继电器
magnetic	有磁性的
flow	流
humidity	湿度
switch	开关
defogger	除雾器
liquid	液态的
steam	气态的
aerosol	雾状
circulate	循环
valve	阀

Phrases(词组)

expansion valve	膨胀阀
blower speed control switch	鼓风机转速控制开关
evaporator temp switch	蒸发器温度开关
low pressure switch	低压开关
A/C magnetic clutch	空调电磁离合器
condenser fan	冷凝器风扇
blower resistor	鼓风机电阻
high pressure switch	高压开关
A/C relay	空调继电器
blower motor	鼓风机电动机
J/B(Junction Block)	连接器盒

Exercises(练习)

1. 根据课文内容回答下列问题

(1) 课文的电路图中有_____不同的搭铁点。

   A. 1个   B. 2个   C. 3个   D. 4个

(2) 鼓风机有_____挡位。

   A. 1个   B. 2个   C. 3个   D. 4个

(3) 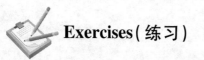 代表_____。

   A. 常闭式继电器   B. 常开式继电器   C. 双掷式继电器

(4) 代表_____。

   A. 电阻丝   B. 变阻器   C. 热敏电阻   D. 传感器

(5) 电路图中有_____熔断丝的容量最大。

   A. AM1   B. GAUGE   C. HTR   D. ALT

2. 将电路图中的导线颜色翻译成中文

English	Chinese	English	Chinese
B		BR	

Chapter 4 Automobile Electric

W _____	O _____
GR _____	L _____
R _____	B-Y _____
P _____	L-W _____

3. 英译汉

When the blower switch is set on, the current flows from the HTR fuse to the HTR relay to the A/C fuse to the terminal 3 of the A/C switch. If the A/C switch is turned on, at this time a signal is input into the engine control module. This activates the engine control module and M/G CLT relay. So that current flows from the A/C fuse to M/G CLT relay to A/C magnetic clutch.

_____
_____
_____。

4. 根据课文内容排序

A/C Amplifier   A/C relay   Battery   A/C magnetic clutch
Fuse Box   Compressor   Ground Point

空调电路的电流路径为：

(1)____   (2)____   (3)____   (4)____
(5)____   (6)____   (7)____

Game Time（游戏时间）

老师把写有空调系统组成部件英文名称的卡片发到每个小组的手上，看哪个小组能够在最短的时间内，按照空调制冷剂在空调里面循环的顺序排队站好，所用时间最短的小组获得胜利。

4.5 The Introduction of the Night View Assist System
(夜视辅助系统的介绍)

The new E-class Mercedes-Benz is equipped with the night view assist system. This system provides a visual representation of the road in darkness, with the aim of identifying people, obstructions or other objects before they become visible in the light cone of the conventional driving lights.

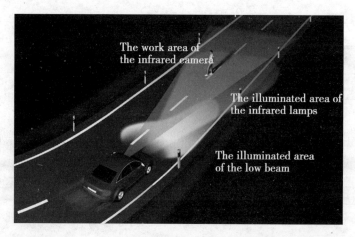

The night view assist system is activated by pressing the night view assist button beside the rotary light switch. In addition, the following function requirements must be fulfilled and registered by the night view assist system control unit:

(1) Rain/light sensor detects darkness.

(2) Rotary light switch in Auto or low beam position.

(3) Reverse gear not engaged.

(4) Vehicle speed above 10 km/h.

When the night view assist system is activated, the road in front of the vehicle is illuminated by two infrared lamps in the front lamp units. If the vehicle is moving forward at a speed less than 5 km/h, the infrared lamps are switched off.

An infrared camera, which is installed behind the windshield in the passenger compartment, scans the illuminated area. The infrared camera of the night view assist system is sensitive to infrared light and designed with a fixed aperture. The picture from the infrared camera is displayed as a black/white video image in the audio/COMAND display. The area displayed corresponds roughly with the area visible through the windshield with the high beam switched on.

A new feature in the night view assist system is the night vision with pedestrian detection function. With this function, any pedestrians detected can be highlighted in the audio/ COMAND display by means of frame corners. The function is intended to make it easier to identify pedestrians especially outside towns on dark country roads. Pedestrians can be detected at ranges up to 90 m in front of the vehicle.

In addition to the function requirements listed above, a prerequisite for night vision with pedestrian detection is that the multifunction camera in the windshield, which is located on the left side of the night view assist camera, must register darkness.

NOTICE:
The light emitted by the infrared lamps is not visible to the human eye. So it does not disturb or dazzle oncoming traffic. The infrared light can therefore remain switched on permanently in addition to the low beam.

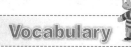

New Words(生词)

cone	光锥体
conventional	传统的
windshield	风窗玻璃
aperture	光圈
video	视频
disturb	打扰
dazzle	炫目

Phrases(词组)

night view assist system	夜视辅助系统
rain/light sensor	雨量/光线传感器
reverse gear	倒挡齿轮
infrared lamp	红外线灯
infrared camera	红外摄像机
passenger compartment	乘客舱

Exercises(练习)

1. 根据课文内容回答下列问题

(1)夜视辅助系统的作用是什么?

────────────────────────

(2)在什么条件下,夜视辅助系统才能被激活?

────────────────────────

(3)夜视辅助系统装备哪些特殊部件?

────────────────────────

(4)简述夜视辅助系统的工作原理。

────────────────────────

2. 英译汉

The light emitted by the infrared lamps is not visible to the human eye. So it does not disturb or dazzle oncoming traffic. The infrared light can therefore remain switched on permanently in addition to the low beam.

Reading Material(阅读材料)

Negotiation of Price

Conversation 1

A: How much is this new model 675?

B: It's 465000 Yuan.

A: I like this car very much but it's a bit expensive for me. Can you give me discount?

B: Well, this is the newest model and very popular. I think it's worth.

A: OK, I'll think about it.

Conversation 2

A: You could save a lot if you would order a little more.

B: How could we do that?

A: We offer a discount for large orders.

B: Let me take another look at our requirements.

Conversation 3

A: We can offer a 10% discount for orders over 10000 pieces.

B: I'm not sure we can use that many.

A: It would represent quite a savings.

B: OK, I'll see what I can do.

对话 1

A:这辆新款的 675 多少钱?

B:465000 元。

A:噢。我很喜欢这辆车,但价钱有点贵,能打折吗?

B:这是最新款,而且非常受欢迎。我觉得这个价钱很合理。

A:好吧,我再考虑一下。

对话 2

A:如果你多订一点,可以省下不少钱。

B:怎么说呢?

A:我们对大量订购有折扣。

B:那我得看看我们的需求量了。

对话 3

A:订购 10000 个以上,我们可以打九折。

B:我怕我们用不了那么多。

A:这省下的可是一笔不少的钱哩。

B:好吧,我考虑考虑吧。

Conversation 4

A: Why are there three prices quoted for this part?

B: They represent the prices for different quantities.

A: I see.

B: The more you order, the more you will save.

对话 4

A：这种零件为什么有 3 种不同的报价？

B：不同的量有不同的价钱。

A：原来如此。

B：订购越多，优惠越多。

Chapter 5 Automobile Maintenance and Testing

(汽车维护与测试)

5.1 General Maintenance

(日常维护)

1. General Notes

Performing the following maintenance checks on the vehicle is the owner's responsibility. In most cases, special tools are not required.

Maintenance requirements vary depending on the country.

Check the maintenance schedule in the owner's manual supplement. Following the maintenance schedule is mandatory.

Determine the appropriate time to service the vehicle using either miles driven or months elapsed, whichever reaches the specification first.

Maintain similar intervals between periodic maintenance, unless otherwise noted.

Failing to check each vehicle part could lead to poor engine performance and increase exhaust emissions.

2. Outside Vehicle

(1) Tires.

①Check the tire inflation pressure with a gauge. Make adjustments if necessary.

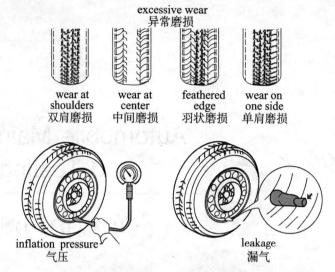

②Check the surfaces of the tires for cuts, damage or excessive wear.

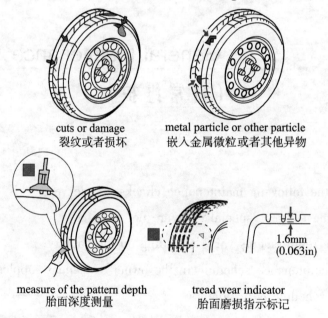

(2) Wheel nuts.

Check for nuts that are loose or missing. Tighten them if necessary.

(3) Windshield wiper blades.

Check the blades for wear or cracks whenever they are unable to wipe the windshield clean. Replace them if necessary.

(4) Fluid leaks.

Check under the vehicle for leaking fuel, oil, water and other fluids.

(5) Doors and engine hood.

Chapter 5   Automobile Maintenance and Testing

①Check that all of the doors and the hood operate smoothly and that all the latches lock securely.

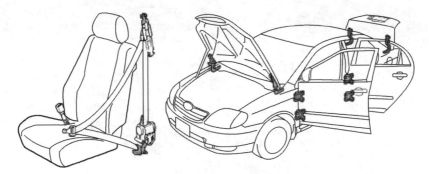

②When the primary latch is released, check that the engine hood secondary latch prevents the hood from opening.

3. Inside Vehicle

(1) Lights.

①Check that the headlights, stop lights, taillights, turn signal lights, and other lights illuminate or blink properly. Also, check if they have enough brightness.

②Check that the headlights are aimed properly.

(2) Warning lights, buzzers and horns.

①Check that all the warning lights and buzzers are working.

②Check that the horn is working.

(3) Windshield wipers and washer.

①Check that the windshield washers are aimed properly. Also, check that the center stream of washer fluid sprays on the windshield within the operating range of the wipers.

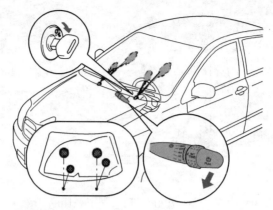

②Check if the wipers streak or not.

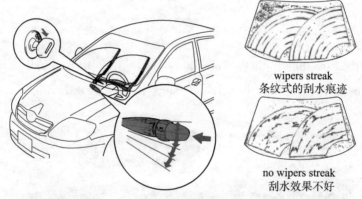

wipers streak
条纹式的刮水痕迹

no wipers streak
刮水效果不好

(4) Windshield defroster.

When the heater or air conditioning is on the defroster setting, check if air comes out of the defroster outlet.

(5) Steering wheel.

Check that the steering wheel has the proper amount of free play. Also check for steering difficulty, free play in the steering wheel and unusual noises.

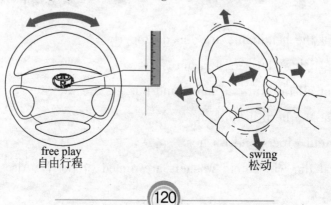

free play
自由行程

swing
松动

(6) Accelerator pedal.

Check that the accelerator pedal operates smoothly. In other words, check that the pedal does not have uneven pedal resistance or become stuck in certain positions.

(7) Brake pedal.

①Check that the brake pedal operates smoothly.

②Check that the pedal has the proper reserve distance and free play.

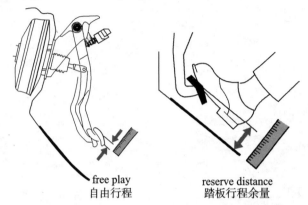

free play
自由行程

reserve distance
踏板行程余量

③Start the engine and check the brake booster function.

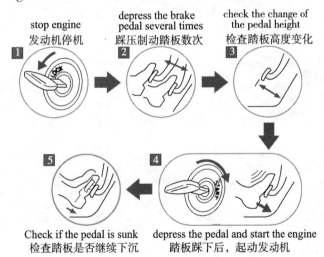

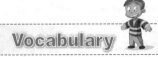

Vocabulary

New Words(生词)

maintenance   维护

tool	工具
emission	排放
hood	罩,盖
latch	门扣
defroster	除霜器

Phrases(词组)

periodic maintenance	定期维护
inflation pressure	充气压力
engine hood	发动机舱盖
air conditioning	空调
free play	自由间隙
accelerator pedal	加速踏板
brake pedal	制动踏板
brake booster	制动助力器

Exercises(练习)

1. 英译汉

(1) Determine the appropriate time to service the vehicle using either miles driven or months elapsed, whichever reaches the specification first.

(2) Failing to check each vehicle part could lead to poor engine performance and increase exhaust emissions.

(3) When the heater or air conditioning is on the defroster setting, check if air comes out of the defroster outlet.

Chapter 5 Automobile Maintenance and Testing

(4) When the primary latch is released, check that the engine hood secondary latch prevents the hood from opening.

2. 根据课文内容,回答下列问题

(1) 在对轮胎做维护时,需要完成哪些项目?

(2) 在什么情况下需要更换刮水器片?

(3) 哪些灯光需要检查照射亮度,哪些灯光需要检查照射位置?

(4) 检查加速踏板和制动踏板的步骤有什么差异?

3. 根据中文提示,用方框里的词填空,组成汽车术语

> wheel brake accelerator booster conditioning defroster light hood

(1) 空调　　air _____
(2) 制动踏板　_____ pedal
(3) 加速踏板　_____ pedal
(4) 警告灯　　warning _____
(5) 发动机舱盖　engine _____
(6) 车窗除霜器　windshield _____
(7) 转向轮　　steering _____
(8) 制动助力器　brake _____

Word-learning Techniques（记词技巧）

👍音译记忆——英语中有些单词广泛被人们用其译音直接称呼,如 engine-引擎(发动机)、jacket-夹克(外套)、cigar-雪茄(香烟)、coffee-咖啡等。我们对待这种译音词的时候,可以直接获得词义。

尝试对下列单词发音,感觉一下它们分别是方框中哪一个物件的直译音。

A. 轮胎　B. 小型卡车　C. 吉普车　D. 电动机　E. 坦克;箱、槽

单词	读音	词义
(1) jeep [dʒiːp]	音似"吉普"	(　)
(2) pickup ['pikʌp]	音似"皮卡"	(　)
(3) motor ['məutə]	音似"马达"	(　)
(4) tank [tæŋk]	音似"坦克",形似大箱子	(　)
(5) tire ['taiə]	音似"胎"	(　)

5.2 Change Engine Oil and Filter

（更换机油和机油滤清器）

1. Parts Location

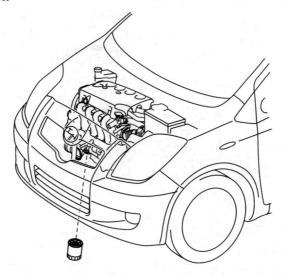

2. Replacement

NOTICE:
Used engine oil contains potentially harmful contaminants which may cause skin cancer. Dispose of used oil and used oil filters at designated disposal sites in order to preserve the environment.

(1) Drain engine oil.

①Remove the oil pan drain plug and drain the engine oil.

②Clean the oil pan drain plug and install it with a new gasket.

Torque: 38 N·m

(2) Remove oil filter sub-assembly.

(3) Install oil filter sub-assembly.

①Check and clean the oil filter installation surface.

②Apply clean engine oil to the gasket of a

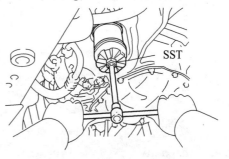

new oil filter.

③Gently screw the oil filter into place, then tighten it until the gasket comes into contact with the seat.

④Using SST, tighten the oil filter sub-assembly.

Torque:13N·m

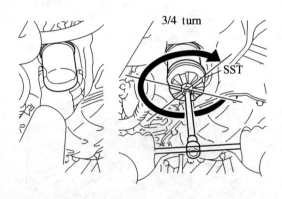

(4) Add engine oil.

①Fill with new engine oil.

Item	Capacity
With oil filter change	3.7 liters
Without oil filter change	3.4 liters
Dry fill	4.1 liters

②Check for engine oil leaks.

③Check engine oil level.

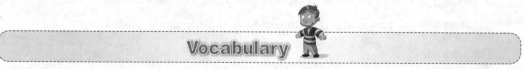

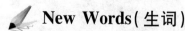

New Words(生词)

screw 旋,拧

capacity 容量

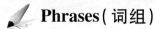

| leak | 泄漏 |
| level | 油面 |

 Phrases(词组)

oil filter   机油滤清器

 Exercises(练习)

1. 英译汉

(1) Used engine oil contains potentially harmful contaminants which may cause skin cancer.

_____。

(2) Apply clean engine oil to the gasket of a new oil filter.

_____。

(3) Gently screw the oil filter into place, then tighten it until the gasket comes into contact with the seat.

_____。

2. 请用中文叙述更换机油和机油滤清器的步骤

_____
_____。

3. 重新加注机油时,如果无须更换机油滤清器,则需要添加多少升机油？在什么情况下需要添加4L机油

_____
_____。

Reading Material(阅读材料)

Regular Maintenance

Conversation	**对话**
Manager: Good morning. What can I do for you?	经理:早上好,有什么需要我帮忙的吗?
Customer: I can't start my car, and I don't know the reason.	顾客:我的汽车不能起动了,不知道是什么原因。
Manager: Have you tried more than once?	经理:您有没有尝试多起动几次?
Customer: Yeah, I have, but failed to get it started.	顾客:是的,尝试了,但还是不行。
Manager: What's your car and where is your location?	经理:您开的是什么车啊?您的位置在哪里?
Customer: My car is a Toyota Corolla and I'm near the Guangzhou Bridge.	顾客:我的车是丰田卡罗拉,我在广州大桥附近。
Manager: OK, we will be there in 10 minutes.	经理:好的,我们10min后赶到。
(after checking)	(检查之后)
Manager: Oh, something wrong with your car's engine and we'd better take your car back to our company to check.	经理:哦,原来是汽车发动机出故障了,我们得拖回厂里检查。
Customer: Oh, that's all right.	顾客:哦,那好吧。

Word-learning Techniques(记词技巧)

词形分析记忆——英文中,有很多英语单词是由下面几种形式构成的:前缀+词根、词根/词干+后缀和前缀+词根/词干+后缀。运用构词法知识,分析单词的词根、前缀、后缀等来记忆单词,对我们会有很大帮助。所谓前缀,就是附加在词根前面的部分。

如单词 intake,其中 in 为前缀,表示"向内"的意思;而 take 为词根,有"接纳"之意,因此该词义为"进入"。又如,单词 output(输出),是给词根 put 加上前缀 out 构成。

下面有一组"前缀 + 词根"构词形式,留意一下其中的基本含义,写出构成的新词。

(1) re(重复,重新) + *turn*(转动)→

(2) pre(前面) + *filter*(过滤)→

(3) counter(相反) + *weight*(重量)→

(4) over(超过) + *head*(头部) →

(5) com(一起) + *press*(压)→

5.3 Diagnosis System(诊断系统)

1. Description

When troubleshooting OBD II (On-Board Diagnostics) vehicles, an intelligent tester must be connected to the DLC3(Data Link Connector 3) of the vehicle. Various data in the vehicle's ECM can be then read.

OBD II regulations require that the vehicle's on-board computer illuminate the MIL(Malfunction Indicator Lamp) on the instrument panel when the computer detects a malfunction in:

a. The emission control system components.

b. The power train control components which affect vehicle emissions.

c. The computer itself.

In order to enhance OBD function on vehicles and develop the Off-Board diagnosis system, CAN(Controller Area Network) communication is introduced in this system. CAN is a network, which uses a pair of data transmission lines, spanning multiple computers and sensors. Since this system is equipped with the CAN communication, connecting the CAN VIM (Vehicle Interface Module) to the intelligent tester is necessary to display any information from the ECM. When confirming the DTCs and any data of the ECM, connect the CAN VIM between the DLC3 and the intelligent tester.

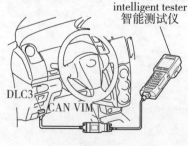

2. Two Trip Detection Logic

When a malfunction is first detected, the malfunction is temporarily stored in the ECM memory (1st trip). If the same malfunction is detected during the next subsequent drive cycle, the MIL is illuminated (2nd trip).

3. Freeze Frame Data

Freeze frame data record the engine conditions (fuel system, calculated engine load, engine coolant temperature, engine speed, etc.) when malfunctions are detected. When troubleshooting, freeze frame data can help determine if the vehicle was moving or stationary, if the engine was warmed up or not, if the air-fuel ratio was lean or rich, and other data from the time the malfunction occurred.

4. MIL (Malfunction Indicator Lamp)

(1) The MIL is illuminated when the ignition switch is first turned on (the engine is not running). If the MIL is not illuminated when the ignition switch is first turned on, check the MIL circuit.

(2) The MIL should turn off when the engine is started. If the MIL remains illuminated, the diagnosis system has detected a malfunction or abnormality in the system.

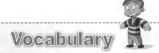

New Words(生词)

malfunction	故障
computer	计算机(电脑)
communication	通信
network	网络
diagnosis	诊断
abnormality	异常

Phrases(词组)

OBD (On-Board Diagnostics)	车载诊断系统

MIL（Malfunction Indicator Lamp） 故障指示灯
VIM（Vehicle Interface Module） 车辆接口模块
freeze frame data 冻结数据帧

Exercises（练习）

1. 翻译短文

Freeze frame data record the engine conditions (fuel system, calculated engine load, engine coolant temperature, engine speed, etc.) when malfunctions are detected. When troubleshooting, freeze frame data can help determine if the vehicle was moving or stationary, if the engine was warmed up or not, if the air-fuel ratio was lean or rich, and other data from the time the malfunction occurred.

2. 根据课文内容，回答下列问题

（1）在检测到什么类型的故障时，车载电脑会点亮仪表板的故障指示灯？

（2）CAN 的作用是什么，在检测带有 CAN 系统的车辆故障时有什么注意事项？

（3）什么是 2 段故障检测逻辑？

（4）故障指示灯的正常工作状态是什么？

Chapter 5 Automobile Maintenance and Testing

Reading Material(阅读材料)

Reply for Customer's Complaints

Conversation	对话
Manager: Hello, This is Sales Department, New Century Automobile Company.	经理:你好,这里是新世纪汽车公司销售部。
Customer: I'm afraid I have to make a complaint with your corporation. It's a most unpleasant incident.	顾客:我得向你们公司提出投诉。这并不是一件令人高兴的事情。
Manager: Oh, what is it about? I'm so sorry to hear that.	经理:什么事? 真遗憾听到此事。
Customer: Yes, I ordered a set of wheel alignment the other day. I received and after I examined them one by one, I found that there must be something wrong with the related computer because it can't give any signal. That's why I want to see the manager.	顾客:确实是这样的,前几天我订购了一台四轮定位仪,等我收到后逐个检查时,我发现配套的计算机屏幕一点信号都没有。这就是我要见经理的原因。
Manager: I am sure everything is all right with that shipment. You see I know you're our regular customer and it is the first time for me to meet with such an inconvenient thing.	经理:我确定那批货的装运一切都是正常的。我知道您是老客户了,我也是第一次遇到这类问题。
Customer: I want to return this.	顾客:我要退货。

Manager: Without sufficient evidence to support, your claim is untenable. If we were at fault, we should be very glad to compensate for your loss.	经理:你必须有足够的证据。如果责任在我方,我们当然乐意赔偿你方损失。
Customer: What's your opinion?	顾客:您的意见如何?
Manager: I'm terribly sorry about that. May I know your name and address, sir? I'll check it and send a repairman to your side at once.	经理:真的很抱歉,请问您的姓名及地址,等我核实后,我会立即派修理工人去你那里处理此事。
Customer: This is Edward Johnson, from No. 120, Rose Avenue.	顾客:我叫爱德华·约翰森,露丝大街120号。

Word-learning Techniques(记词技巧)

👍 词形分析记忆——所谓后缀,就是附加在词根后面的部分。它主要是改变词类,但有时也改变词义。如动词 speak(讲话),它后面加上"er"之后就派生出新词 speaker(扬声器),其词性为名词,表示一种物件。

根据附加后缀派生单词的做法,写出下面各组的新词。

(1) cool(冷却)+ *ing*(形容词形式)→

(2) lubricate(润滑)+ *ing*(形容词形式)→

(3) ignite(点火)+ *tion*(名词形式)→

(4) resist(反抗)+ *ance*(名词形式)→

(5) break(断裂)+ *er*(名词形式,表示某人或物)→

5.4 Data List and Active Test
（数据流和功能测试）

1. Data List

By reading the data list displayed on an intelligent tester, values can be checked, including those of the switches, sensors, and actuators, without removing any parts. Reading the data list as the first step of troubleshooting is one method of shortening diagnostic time.

> **NOTICE:**
> In the table below, the values listed under Normal Condition are for reference only. Do not depend solely on these values when determining whether or not a part is faulty.

(1) Warm up the engine.

(2) Turn the ignition switch to OFF.

(3) Connect the intelligent tester to the DLC3.

(4) Turn the ignition switch to ON.

(5) Turn the tester ON.

(6) Select the following menu items: DIAGNOSIS/ENHANCED OBD Ⅱ/DATA LIST.

(7) Check the values by referring to the table below.

Intelligent Tester Display	Measurement: Range	Normal Condition	Diagnostic Note
Injector	Injection period of No. 1cylinder: Min: 0ms, Max: 32.64ms	1.0 to 3.0 ms: Idling	
IGN Advance	Ignition timing advance for No. 1 cylinder: Min:-64 deg, Max:63.5 deg	BTDC 0 to 14 deg: Idling	

续上表

Intelligent Tester Display	Measurement: Range	Normal Condition	Diagnostic Note

MAF	Air flow rate from MAF meter: Min:0 g/sec, Max:655.35 g/sec	1 to 3 g/sec: Idling
		2 to 6 g/sec: Running without load at 2500rpm
			If value approximately 0 g/sec
			  MAF meter power source circuit open
			If value 160g/sec or more
			  E2G circuit open

Coolant temp	Engine coolant temperature: Min: -40℃, Max: 140℃	80 to 100℃: After warming up	If -40℃: sensor circuit open If 140℃ or more: sensor circuit shorted
Air-fuel ratio	Ratio compared to stoichiometric level: Min: 0, Max: 1.999	0.8 to 1.2: Idling	Less than 1 (0 to 0.99): Lean Greater than 1 (1.001 to 1.999): Rich
…	…	…	…

2. Active Test

Performing an active test enables components including the relays, VSV(Vacuum Switching Valve) and actuators, to be operated without removing any parts. The active test can be performed with an intelligent tester. Performing an active test as the first step of troubleshooting is one method of shortening diagnostic time.

Data list can be displayed during active test.

(1) Connect the intelligent tester to the DLC3.

(2) Turn the ignition switch to ON.

(3) Turn the tester ON.

(4) Select the following menu items: DIAGNOSIS/ENHANCED OBD Ⅱ/ACTIVE TEST.

(5) Perform the ACTIVE TEST by referring to the table below.

Chapter 5　Automobile Maintenance and Testing

Intelligent Tester Display	Test Details	Control Ranges	Diagnostic Notes
INJ VOL	Change injection volume	Between −12.5 and 24.8%	All injectors tested at same time Perform test at less than 3000rpm Injection volume can be changed in 0.1% graduations within control range.
FUEL PUMP/SPD	Activate fuel pump (C/OPN Relay)	ON/OFF	Test possible when engine stopped
COOLING FAN	Control Electric Cooling Fan	ON/OFF	
ETCS CLOSE/ OPEN SLOW	Throttle actuator	ON: Throttle valve closes/opens slowly	Test possible when following conditions met: Engine stopped Shift position in P Fully depressing accelerator pedal
FUEL CUT #1	Cylinder #1 injector fuel cut	ON/OFF	Test possible during vehicle stopping and engine idling
…	…	…	…

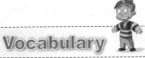

 # New Words(生词)

actuator　　　　　　　　　　　　　　执行器
reference　　　　　　　　　　　　　 参考
circuit　　　　　　　　　　　　　　　电路
lean　　　　　　　　　　　　　　　　稀薄

Phrases(词组)

data list	数据流
active test	动态测试
VSV(Vacuum Switching Valve)	真空开关阀
ETCS(Electronic Throttle Control System)	电子节气门控制系统

Exercises(练习)

1. 翻译短文

By reading the data list displayed on an intelligent tester, values can be checked, including those of the switches, sensors, and actuators, without removing any parts. Reading the data list as the first step of troubleshooting is one method of shortening diagnostic time.

_____

_____

Performing an active test enables components including the relays, VSV(Vacuum Switching Valve) and actuators, to be operated without removing any parts. The active test can be performed with an intelligent tester. Performing an active test as the first step of troubleshooting is one method of shortening diagnostic time.

_____

_____

2. 根据课文内容,回答下列问题
(1)叙述数据流测试的方法步骤。

_____

(2)测试数据流时,发动机在怠速运转工况下,喷油器的喷油时间是多少?

_____

(3)检测 MAF(空气流量计)信号时,如果数据显示 0g/s,则 MAF 可能存在什么故障?

_____

(4)数据流测试和功能测试都有助于故障诊断,两者有何区别?

_____

Reading Material(阅读材料)

Users' Feedback

Conversation	对话
Salesman: Hello, This is New Century Automobile Company. I'm calling to know whether everything has gone well with your computer.	业务员:您好,这里是新世纪汽车公司。不知您的计算机现在运转是否正常。
Customer: Thanks a lot. It works excellently after being repaired.	顾 客:非常感谢,维修之后一切正常。
Salesman: I'm very happy to hear you say so and I do hope the minor problem didn't cause you much inconvenience.	业务员:很高兴听您这么说,但愿这一小问题没给您带来太多不便。
Customer: Thank you very much for your good service. I'm sure your company will be making more money.	顾 客:谢谢你们真诚的服务,我相信贵公司生意会更加红火。

Salesman: It is always our policy to give reliable and satisfactory services to our clients. Let's find out what you like by doing a market research and it will give us an indication.	业务员:给顾客提供优质、满意的服务是我们的宗旨。让我们做个市场调查吧,我想这将帮助公司成长。
Customer: OK, I feel the height of the computer is too high that I have to operate by standing.	顾 客:我认为计算机的高度太高,我只能站着操作。
Salesman: It's a good suggestion. I'll report to the manager right now!	业务员:这是个很好的建议,我会立刻向经理汇报。
Customer: I recommend a pleasant color to match with the house's color.	顾 客:我建议色泽要好看一些,并且与房子的颜色要匹配。
Salesman: Thank you for you warmhearted reply. I feel more optimistic and more confident about our relations in the future.	业务员:谢谢您热情的回答。我对我们未来的合作更加乐观和充满信心。
Customer: It's just my own opinion, I'd like you to think it over.	顾 客:这仅仅是我个人的观点,希望你们能够再考虑一下。
Salesman: We'll go into it further, and let you know what decision we reach.	业务员:我们会做深入的调查,并且把我们的决定告诉您。
Customer: I shall be glad to hear from you.	顾 客:我会很乐意听到你们的决定。
Salesman: Thank you, bye-bye!	业务员:谢谢,再见!
Customer: See you later.	顾 客:再见。

Word-learning Techniques(记词技巧)

 词形分析记忆——词最根本的、不能进一步拆分的部分叫作词根。词根具有词的最基本的意义。而词干指的是加后缀之前词根的变形。通常熟悉某一词根的意义,并了解其前缀、后缀的基本含义,可以大致推测出新词的词义。如:单词 compression,由前缀 com-(一起) + 词根 press(压) + 后缀-ion(名词后缀),该词义很可能被猜作"与压力有关的事"。该词实际上就是"压缩"的意思。

你能认定下面各组的词根或词干(粗斜体)的意义、前缀的含义以及后缀的作用之后,写出派生的新词并猜写它们的词义吗?

(1) auto(自动) + *mob*(移动、运动) + ile(具……性质的)→

(2) op(反、逆) + *pose*(姿势、样子) + ed(表语结构)→

(3) super(超级) + *charge*(承担……任务) + ed(表语结构)→

(4) trans(转变) + *miss*(发出) + ion(名词形式)→

(5) re(再) + *sist*(反抗) + ance(名词形式)→

5.5 The WorldSkills Competition
（世界技能竞赛）

The WorldSkills Competition occurs every two years and is the biggest vocational education and skills excellence event in the world. The competitors represent the best of their peers and are selected from WorldSkills' Member countries and regions. They will demonstrate technical abilities both individually and collectively to execute specific tasks for which they study and will perform in the future.

Competitors for Automobile Technology will be judged on:

- General Competency.
- Electrical Systems Construction and Testing.
- Brake and stability control Systems.
- Suspension and Steering Systems.
- Engine Mechanical Repair.
- Transmissions manual and automatic.
- Diesel systems.
- Engine management.
- Diagnostics.
- Good understanding and interpretation of electrical and network diagram, work with modern computer based diagnostic systems.
- Ability to measure and interpret at electrical harnesses on modern cars.
- Ability to search information on OL workshop manual, interpret Diagnostic Trouble Codes DTC's.

COMPETITOR INSTRUCTIONS

Module A-Engine management Systems

Equipment: Ford Fusion EcoBoost

Module duration: 3 Hours

Instructions

Criteria A1 and A2 must be completed in order shown below. A3 and A4 can be

Chapter 5　Automobile Maintenance and Testing

completed in any order. Any identified faults are to be reported to the Expert. The expert will advise the correct repair action to be taken by the competitor.

A1	The engine will not rotate. Make all necessary repairs that allows the engine to rotate. The scan tool cannot be used to perform this part of your test. **Note**: You have 80 minutes to complete this part of the Module. If you fail to get the engine rotating you will be sent to the competitor's room for a imposed ten minute penalty. The Experts will rectify the faults, after ten minutes the competitor will return to begin work on A2. The competitor will be awarded marks for any faults found in A1
A2	The engine will not run, make all the necessary repairs to enable the engine to run without any faults. All diagnostic equipment is available. **Note**: You have 60 minutes to complete Criteria A2. If you fail to get the engine running correctly with no faults present you will be sent to the competitors room for a imposed ten minute penalty. The Experts will rectify the faults, after ten minutes the competitor will return to begin work on Criteria A3 and A4. The competitor will be awarded marks for any faults found in A2
A3	Complete all requirements on . A3 report sheet
A4	Complete all requirements on . A4 report sheet

Module B - Steering Brake Suspension Systems

Equipment: Toyota Corolla

Module duration: 3 Hours

Instructions

B4 must be performed last.

B1	Complete the task according to industry standards
B2	Replace shock absorber front left Replace lower ball joint front left Replace tie rod end front left Replace lower arm front right
B3	Replace front left brake calliper Replace flexible brake hose front left Check and repair the ABS
B4	Perform a 4 wheel alignment according to manufactures specifications Print out the final report sheet

Module C – Electrical and Electronic Systems

Equipment: VW Tiguan

Module duration: 3 Hours

Instructions

C2 has to be done before moving to next task, competitor can shift between C3 – C6 as many times he/she likes. When going to C7 no return to tasks C3-C6 is allowed!

C1	Complete task according to industry standards
C2	Complete the wiring diagrams so that the correct function are achieved and meet industrial standards. Maximum time 30min
C3	Check function of all gauges – instruments. Advise expert of faults before repair
C4	Check all external lights on the car, advise expert before repairing faults. Fill out report sheet with the correct values
C5	Check all door operations, advice expert before repair of faults. Perform a measurement on CAN-high comfort system, freeze screen on tool when you are satisfied and show expert before moving on
C6	Check complete wiper functions, advise expert before repair of faults. Perform a measurement on LIN signal (wiper system, freeze screen on tool when you are satisfied and show expert before moving on
C7	Check fault codes with diagnostic tool, reset fault codes and inform expert of result

Module D-Engine Mechanical

Equipment: PSA 1.6L 16 Valve Direct Injection Turbocharged

Module duration: 3 Hours

Instructions

All work to be completed in the order below.

D1	Perform cylinder leakage test on all cylinders and record results
D2	Dismantle engine
D3	Perform measurements on report sheets
D4	Determine serviceability of components
D5	Reassemble engine
D6	Perform all work according to industry standards

Chapter 5 Automobile Maintenance and Testing

Module E-Drive Line

Equipment：VW Transmission MQ25 6F

Module duration：3 Hours

Instructions

All work to be completed in the order below.

E1	Complete the task according to industry standards
E2	Disassemble the Transmission
E3	Perform inspection and measurements of the transaxle according to the report sheet
E4	Assembly the MT and carry out adjustment as required by the manufacturer
E5	Measurement and faults must be shown to the Expert

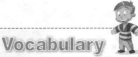

New Words（生词）

automatic	自动
diesel	柴油机
scan	扫描
rectify	去除
caliper	卡钳

Phrases（词组）

CAN（Controller Area Network）	控制器局域网络
LIN（Local Interconnect Network）	局域互联网络

Exercises（练习）

1. 翻译短文

It is the first time in history that the WorldSkills Competition will be held in

South America. The 43rd edition, being held in São Paulo in August 2015, is expected to surpass the record number of Competitors registered for the Competition. In Leipzig, Germany in 2013-nearly 1,000 participants from 53 countries and regions competed for medals in 46 Skills.

———————————————————————————

———————————————————————————

———————————————————————————

2. 根据课文内容,回答下列问题
(1)世界技能竞赛汽车技术竞赛项目考核参赛者哪些能力?

———————————————————————————

(2)模块 A 的 A1、A2 部分的故障排除工作有何不同?

———————————————————————————

(3)模块 B 的 B2 部分需要完成哪些工作?

———————————————————————————

(4)模块 C 在检查外部灯之前需要完成什么工作?

———————————————————————————

(5)分别叙述模块 D、E 的工作步骤。

———————————————————————————

Extend Reading(拓展阅读)

The WorldSkills Competition

It is the first time in history that the WorldSkills Competition will be held in South America. The 43rd edition, being held in São Paulo in August 2015, is expected to surpass the record number of Competitors registered for the Competition. In Leipzig, Germany in 2013-nearly 1000 participants from 53 countries and regions competed for medals in 46 Skills.

Appendices
（附录）

Ⅰ Measuring Tools(各种工具量具)

线性测量工具(linear measuring tools)

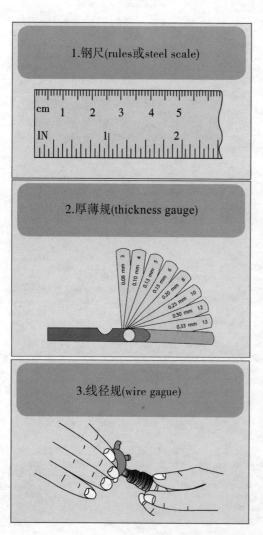

1. 钢尺(rules或steel scale)

2. 厚薄规(thickness gauge)

3. 线径规(wire gague)

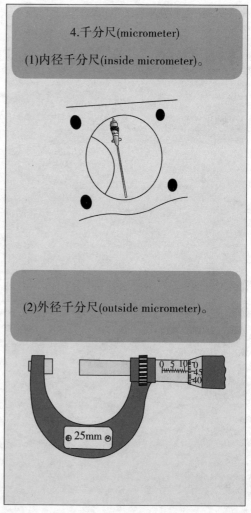

4. 千分尺(micrometer)

(1)内径千分尺(inside micrometer)。

(2)外径千分尺(outside micrometer)。

Appendices

5.百分表(dial gauge)

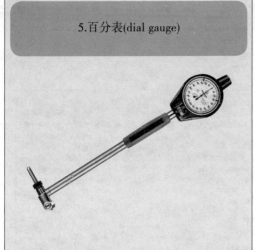

6.量缸表(cylinder-bore gauge)

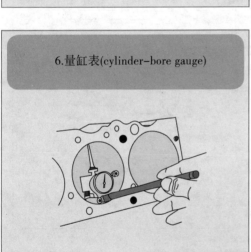

7.深度规(depth gauge)

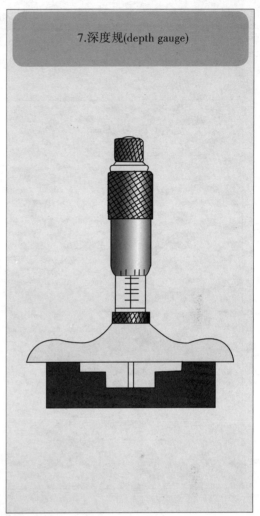

8.游标卡尺(veriner caliper)

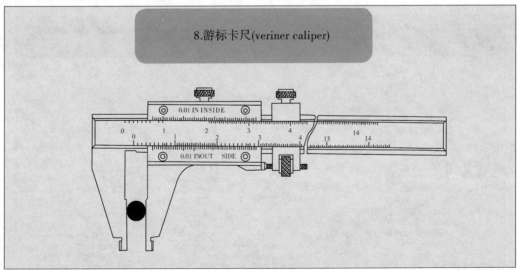

手动工具(Hand tools)

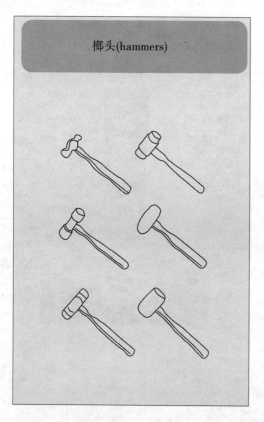

榔头(hammers)

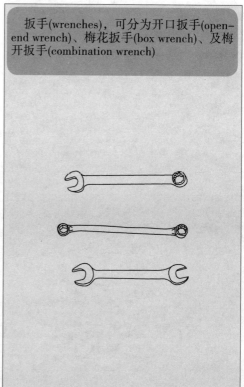

扳手(wrenches)，可分为开口扳手(open-end wrench)、梅花扳手(box wrench)、及梅开扳手(combination wrench)

螺丝刀(screwdrivers),可分为一字螺丝刀(slot-head scerwdivers)及十字螺丝刀(phillips-head screwdrivers)

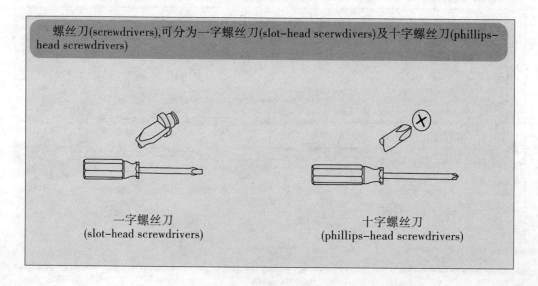

一字螺丝刀
(slot-head screwdrivers)

十字螺丝刀
(phillips-head screwdrivers)

油管扳手(flare-nut wrench)

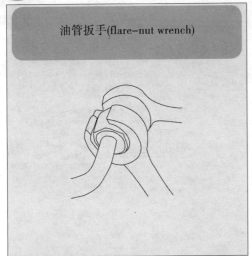

活动扳手(adjustable wrench)

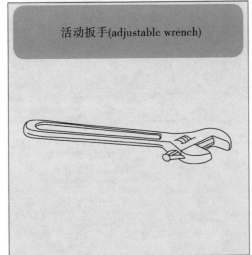

扭力扳手(torque wrench)

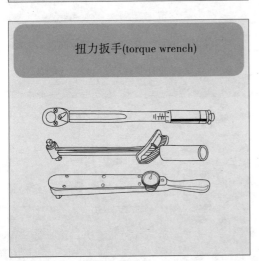

夹持钳(gripping pliers)

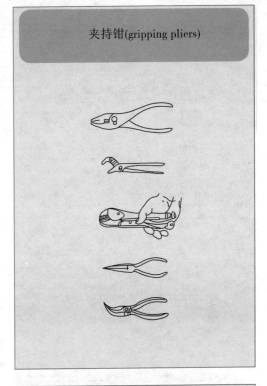

剪切钳(cutting pliers)

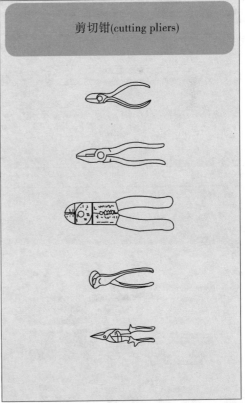

螺柱拔取器(stud extractor)

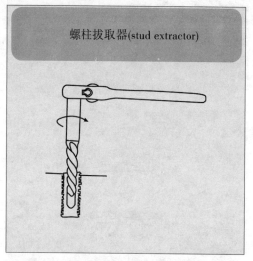

手工锯(hacksaw)

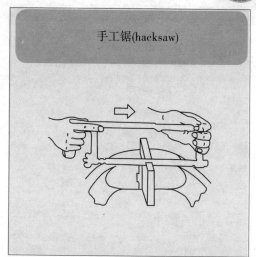

凿刀(chisels)

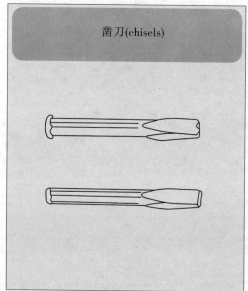

冲销(punches)

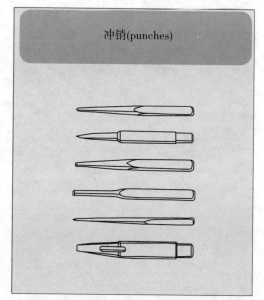

锉刀(files)

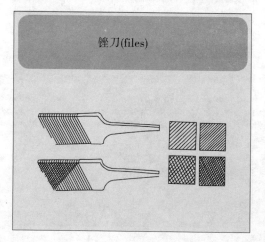

切管器(tubing cutter)

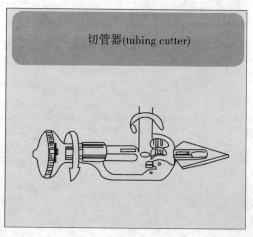

电动工具(electric tools)

电钻(electric drill)

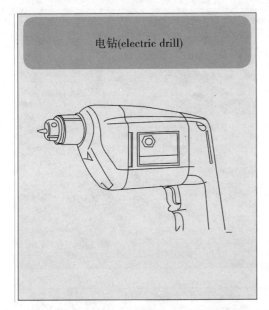

电烙铁(soldering gun)

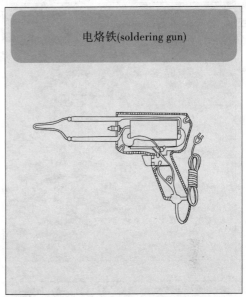

砂轮机(grinder)

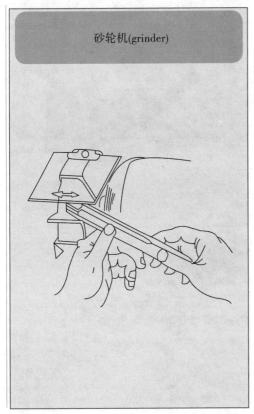

钻床(drill press)

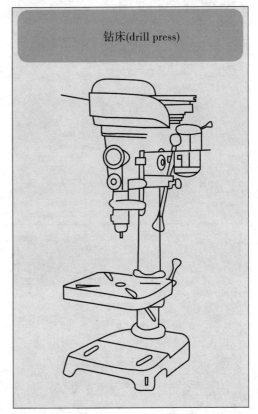

气动工具(pneumatic tools)

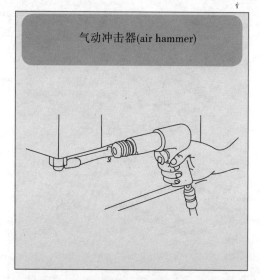
气动冲击器(air hammer)

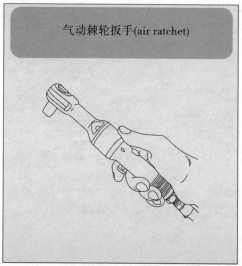
气动棘轮扳手(air ratchet)

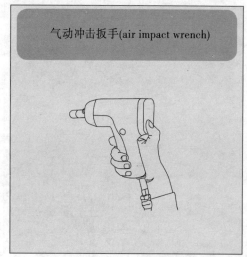
气动冲击扳手(air impact wrench)

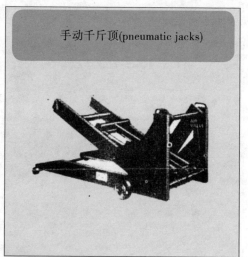
手动千斤顶(pneumatic jacks)

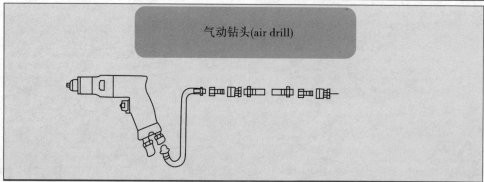
气动钻头(air drill)

液压工具(hydraulic tools)

液压千斤顶(hydraulic jack)

液压压床(hydraulic press)

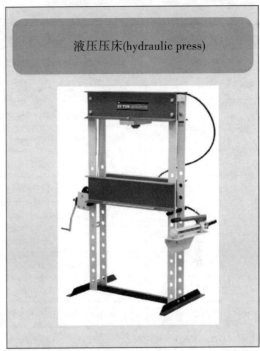

吊车(shop crane)

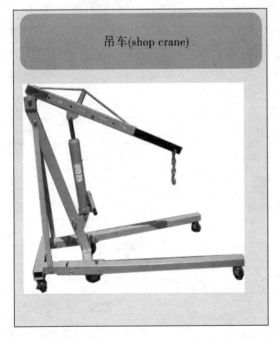

举升机(lifter)

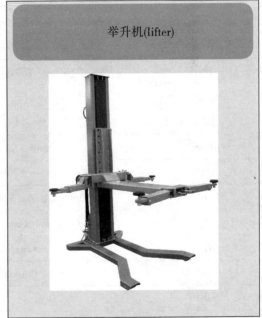

Ⅱ Abbreviations for Automobile(汽车常用缩略语)

Abbreviations	English Term	Chinese Term
ABS	Anti-Lock Brake System	防抱死制动系统
A/C	Air Conditioner	空调
AC	Alternating Current	交流电
ACC	Accessory	附件
ACIS	Acoustic Control Induction System	声控进气系统
A/F	Air-Fuel Ratio	空燃比
AHC	Active Height Control Suspension	主动高度可调悬架
ALT	Alternator	发电机
AMP	Amplifier	放大器
ANT	Antenna	天线
ASD	Automatic Locking Differential	自动差速锁装置
ASSY	Assembly	总成
A/T	Automatic Transmission	自动变速器
ATF	Automatic Transmission Fluid	自动变速器油
AVS	Adaptive Variable Suspension	自适应可变悬架
B+	Battery Voltage	蓄电池电压
BAS	Brake Assist System	制动辅助系统
BDC	Bottom Dead Center	下止点
B/S	Bore-Stroke Ratio	缸径冲程比
CAN	Controller Area Network	控制器区域网络
CRS	Child Restraint System	儿童约束系统
CKP	Crankshaft Position	曲轴位置
CC	Cruise Control	巡航系统
DC	Direct Current	直流电
DEF	Defogger	除雾器
DLC	Data Link Connector	数据传输器连接器
DOHC	Double Overhead Camshaft	双顶置凸轮轴

续上表

Abbreviations	English Term	Chinese Term
DTC	Diagnostic Trouble Code	诊断故障代码
EBD	Electric Brake Force Distribution	电子制动力分配
ECT	Engine Coolant Temperature	发动机冷却液温度
ECU	Electronic Control Unit	电子控制单元
EFI	Electronic Fuel Injection	电子燃油喷射
EGR	Exhaust Gas Recirculation	废气再循环
EPS	Electric Power Steering	电子助力转向
ESA	Electronic Spark Advance	电子点火提前
ESP	Electronic Stability Program	电控车辆稳定行驶系统
EVAP	Evaporative Emission Control System	燃油挥发排放控制装置
FP	Fuel Pump	燃油泵
GAS	Gasoline	汽油
GND	Ground	搭铁
GPS	Global Positioning System	全球定位系统
IAT	Intake Air Temperature	进气温度
IC	Instrument Cluster	仪表盘
IG	Ignition	点火
ISC	Idle Speed Control	怠速自动调节
J/B	Junction Block	接线盒
KS	Knock Sensor	爆震传感器
LAN	Local Area Network	局域网
LED	Light Emitting Diode	发光二极管
LPG	Liquefied Petroleum Gas	液化石油气
MAF	Mass Air Flow Sensor	空气质量流量传感器
MAP	Manifold Absolute Pressure	歧管绝对压力
MIL	Malfunction Indicator Light	故障指示灯
MT	Manual Transmission	手动变速器
NTC	Negative Temperature Coefficient	负温度系数
O2S	Oxygen Sensor	氧传感器
OHC	Overhead Camshaft	顶置凸轮轴
PCV	Positive Crankcase Ventilation	曲轴箱强制通风

续上表

Abbreviations	English Term	Chinese Term
PTC	Positive Temperature Coefficient	正温度系数
PW	Power Windows	电动车窗
RAM	Random Access Memory	随机存储器
R/B	Relay Block	继电器盒
ROM	Read Only Memory	只读存储器
SC	Supercharger	增压器
SPI	Single Point Injection	单点喷射
SRS	Supplemental Restraint System	辅助约束系统
SST	Special Service Tools	专用工具
TBI	Throttle Body Electronic Fuel Injection	节气门体电子燃油喷射
TDC	Top Dead Center	上止点
TWC	Three-Way Catalyst	三元催化器
VIN	Vehicle Identification Number	车辆识别码
VSS	Vehicle Speed Signal	车速信号
VSV	Vacuum Switching Valve	真空转换阀
VVT-i	Variable Valve Timing-intelligent	智能可变气门正时
4WD	Four Wheel Drive	四轮驱动

参 考 文 献

[1] 武华.汽车发动机构造与拆装工作页[M].2版.北京:人民交通出版社,2013.

[2] 武华.汽车底盘构造与拆装工作页[M].2版.北京:人民交通出版社,2007.

[3] 赵金明,林振江.汽车实用英语[M].北京:人民交通出版社,2011.

[4] 王会,刘朝红.汽车发动机构造与维修[M].北京:人民交通出版社,2010.

[5] 高元伟,吕学前.汽车底盘构造与维修[M].北京:人民交通出版社,2010.

人民交通出版社汽车类中职教材部分书目

一、全国交通运输职业教育教学指导委员会规划教材 教育部中等职业教育汽车专业技能课教材

书号	书名	作者	定价	出版时间	课件
978-7-114-12216-3	汽车文化	李 青、刘新江	38.00	2017.03	有
978-7-114-12517-1	汽车定期维护	陆松波	39.00	2017.03	有
978-7-114-12170-8	汽车机械基础	何向东	37.00	2017.03	有
978-7-114-12648-2	汽车电工电子基础	陈文均	36.00	2017.03	有
978-7-114-12241-5	汽车发动机机械维修	杨建良	25.00	2017.03	有
978-7-114-12383-2	汽车传动系统维修	曾 丹	22.00	2017.03	有
978-7-114-12369-6	汽车悬架、转向与制动系统维修	郭碧宝	31.00	2017.03	有
978-7-114-12371-9	汽车发动机电器与控制系统检修	姚秀驰	33.00	2017.03	有
978-7-114-12314-6	汽车车身电气设备检修	占百春	22.00	2017.03	有
978-7-114-12467-9	汽车发动机及底盘常见故障的诊断与排除	杨永先	25.00	2017.03	有
978-7-114-12428-0	汽车自动变速器维修	王 健	23.00	2017.03	有
978-7-114-12225-5	汽车网络控制系统检修	毛叔平	29.00	2017.03	有
978-7-114-12193-7	新能源汽车结构与检修	陈社会	38.00	2017.03	有
978-7-114-12209-5	汽车检测与诊断技术	蒋红梅、吴国强	26.00	2017.03	有
978-7-114-12565-2	汽车检测设备的使用与维护	刘宣传、梁 钢	27.00	2017.03	有
978-7-114-12374-0	汽车维修接待实务	王彦峰	30.00	2017.06	有
978-7-114-12392-4	汽车保险与理赔	荆叶平	32.00	2017.06	有
978-7-114-12177-7	汽车维修基础	杨承明	26.00	2017.03	有
978-7-114-12538-6	汽车商务礼仪	赵 颖	32.00	2017.06	有
978-7-114-12442-6	汽车销售流程	李雪婷	30.00	2017.06	有
978-7-114-12488-4	汽车配件基础知识	杨二杰	20.00	2017.03	有
978-7-114-12546-1	汽车配件管理	吕 琪	33.00	2017.03	有
978-7-114-12539-3	客户关系管理	喻 媛	30.00	2017.06	有
978-7-114-12446-4	汽车电子商务	李 晶	30.00	2017.03	有
978-7-114-13054-0	汽车使用与维护	李春生	28.00	2017.04	有
978-7-114-12382-5	机械识图	林治平	24.00	2017.03	有
978-7-114-12804-2	汽车车身电气系统拆装	张 炜	35.00	2017.03	有
978-7-114-12190-6	汽车材料	陈 虹	29.00	2017.03	有
978-7-114-12466-2	汽车钣金工艺	林育彬	37.00	2017.03	有
978-7-114-12286-6	汽车车身与附属设备	胡建富、马 涛	22.00	2017.03	有
978-7-114-12315-3	汽车美容	赵俊山	20.00	2017.03	有
978-7-114-12144-9	汽车构造	齐忠志	39.00	2017.03	有
978-7-114-12262-0	汽车涂装基础	易建红	30.00	2017.04	有
978-7-114-13290-2	汽车美容与装潢经营	邵伟军	28.00	2017.04	有

二、中等职业教育国家规划教材

书号	书名	作者	定价	出版时间	课件
978-7-114-12992-6	机械基础（少学时）（第二版）	刘新江、袁 亮	34.00	2016.06	有
978-7-114-12872-1	汽车电控发动机构造与维修（第三版）	王 囤	32.00	2016.06	有
978-7-114-12902-5	汽车发动机构造与维修（第三版）	张 嫣、苏 畅	35.00	2016.05	有
978-7-114-12812-7	汽车底盘构造与维修（第三版）	王家青、孟华霞、陆志琴	39.00	2016.04	有
978-7-114-12903-2	汽车电气设备构造与维修（第三版）	周建平	43.00	2016.05	有
978-7-114-12820-2	汽车自动变速器构造与维修（第三版）	周志伟、韩彦明、顾雯斌	29.00	2016.04	有
978-7-114-12845-5	汽车使用性能与检测（第三版）	杨益明、郭 彬	25.00	2016.04	有
978-7-114-12684-0	汽车材料（第三版）	周 燕	31.00	2016.01	有

咨询电话：010-85285962；010-85285977. 咨询QQ：616507284；99735898